Winning Strategies

for

B2B E-Commerce

The IQ Guides collection focuses on change. They are practically oriented and have been developed in line with scientific concepts and studies. These texts help readers develop informed strategies for such change based on their particular situations. We look forward to your comments and questions. Please feel free to contact us.

VALLIER LAPIERRE

WINNING
STRATEGIES

FOR

B2B E-COMMERCE

IQGuides

Canadian Cataloguing in Publication Data
Lapierre Vallier, 1948-
Winning strategies for B2B E-Commerce
(IQ Guides)
Translation of: Pour un commerce électronique entre entreprises gagnantes.
Includes bibliographical references.
ISBN 2-922417-20-4
1. Electronic commerce. 2. Internet marketing. 3. Electronic data interchange. 4. Small business.
5. Electronic commerce – Canada. I. Title. II. Series.
HF5548.32.L36813 2001   658.8'00285'4678   C2001-940236-8

Legal deposit
Bibliothèque nationale du Québec
National Library of Canada

Distributed in North America by:
General Distribution Services
325 Humber College Blvd
Toronto (Ontario) H9W 7C3
Telephone : (416) 213-1919
http://www.genpub.com

Distributed in Europe by:
Gazelle Book Services
Queen Square
Lancaster LA1 1RN United Kingdom
Telephone : 01 524 68765
http://www.gazellebooks.co.uk

Project Coordinator: Danièle Lajeunesse, Electronic Commerce Institute
Reviewer: Yves Leclerc
Consultants: Jean-René Carron, Pascal Raymond, Claude Riopel, Electronic Commerce Institute,
and Diane Provencher, Treasury Board of Canada Secretariat
Translation: Josh Wallace
Editor: Marie-Hélène Crémer
Quizzes: Bernard Dubreuil
Revision: Maryse Tardif
Proofreader: Élyse Leconte
Illustrations: Christiane Beauregard
Layout: Trait d'union

© Isabelle Quentin éditeur, 2001
http://iqe.qc.ca
ISBN 2-922417-20-4   1 2 3 4 5 05 04 03 02 01

TABLE OF CONTENTS

FOREWORD

Winning Strategies for B2B E-Commerce offers a detailed roadmap of the trends that have been emerging since early 1999 in business-to-business electronic commerce. Senior author Vallier Lapierre focuses on the development of electronic auctions, e-marketplaces, the outsourcing of technologies by application service providers (ASPs) and the evolution of a cooperative structure that governs all of these processes.

This guide aims to provide an overview, rather than a portrait frozen in time, of the ever-changing world of B2B e-commerce in which one innovation is always ready to supplant another. We should never make the mistake of trying to freeze-frame the process of change to make it easier to assess the upheavals in our lives since the dawn of the Internet.

We believe that while this book may not assuage all of the concerns of the small business leaders to whom it is addressed, it will help many understand how B2B e-commerce works and thus help them make critical decisions in this area. We are therefore very proud to have helped produce this work, as part of our goal of providing the training and heightened awareness that will encourage small business to become part of the electronic business community.

I would also like to acknowledge the financial support of the Quebec Conseil du Trésor, QuébecTel, Canada Economic Development and the Canada Development Bank, all of which helped mobilize so much energy around this project. We are grateful to these organizations for having substantially improved our working conditions. In particular, their support permitted us to obtain a much broader view of these constantly evolving issues as it enabled us to closely monitor them for nearly one year.

We would also like to thank publisher Isabelle Quentin (IQ).

We shall continue to keep a close watch on developments in the world of e-business. In the meantime, we hope you enjoy—and profit from—this guide.

Pierre Langelier

President and CEO of the Electronic Commerce Institute

INTRODUCTION

The idea for this book originated in the article "PME du monde entier, unissez-vous" (Small Businesses of the World, Unite!), published on the Clés du commerce électronique Web site[1] on November 21, 1997. This manual and the article were both designed to help small business heads and self-employed workers find ways to take advantage of the upheavals occurring in all spheres of economic activity, including government, through the advent of a knowledge-based society. No one can fully anticipate the impact of the gradual shift by all B2B information exchanges to the Internet, so we cannot set out a roadmap that will guarantee small business easy access to this new kingdom.

However, by early 1999, the near-team impact of B2B e-commerce on Quebec and Canadian small businesses was already clearly visible, based on changes then occurring in the U.S. and which could be expected to take one to two years to percolate through to here. This watch south of the border should prove useful in guiding our businesses on what to expect by 2001 in the world of ecommerce. In any event, e-commerce is already getting rooted" here, as is particularly apparent in our chapters on e-marketplaces and Internet-based outsourcing of software applications.

Naturally, such trends will occur locally on a smaller scale, but they should maintain the same pace set in the United States. U.S. excitement for B2B e-commerce suffered a setback, of course, following mid-2000's big stock market losses—also felt here—among new dot-com shares.

---

1 www.cles.ca

This slowdown gave companies time to catch their collective breath, while staying on course in their new efforts.

Still, this does not mean that any of the main U.S. e-commerce practices will not simply fade away at some point. E-marketplaces, online auctions, Internet-based outsourcing of IT and telecom applications are some of the major phenomena that may or may not prove their mettle over time. An article appearing in the December 2000 *Harvard Business Review* says peer-to-peer communications, epitomized by Napster, are likely to cut into the popularity of B2B e-marketplaces, which still managed to monopolize attention throughout 2000.

The recession into which it appears we may be heading (as we go to press), will, however, only put a slight brake on these trends in both the U.S. and Canada, since economic slowdowns are always propitious to improving business operations—which in this case means taking a keener interest in B2B e-commerce. Ultimately, the progress companies make in this area will depend on the overall situation.

This also means we can take with a grain of salt the forecasts of U.S. research firms concerning the growth in ecommerce-based B2B trade. Gartner Group, Forrester Research, Yankee Group, Jupiter Communications and brokerages like Morgan Stanley Dean Witter, Bear Stearns and Merrill Lynch have almost universally predicted such trade will be worth from $3 to $6 trillion internationally in 2004. Most of these projections were made before Internet share prices—bloated largely from the exuberance of these forecasters—burst. These estimates nonetheless point out and inevitable trend, even were we to allow for a one or two-year delay in their kick-off.

Whatever the circumstances, B2B e-commerce might create more losers than winners among existing small businesses. Quite a few will miss the boat entirely and disappear if they are not lucky enough to get bought out. But we could also argue that the importance of small business to the New Economy could still maintain itself—or even increase, since B2B e-commerce could ultimately result in the creation of as many or even more new small businesses as are lost in the transition.

Because the Internet makes it far easier for companies to outsource their non-core specialities, it will certainly lead to geometric growth in subcontracting in all existing and future fields of business. This market is within reach of the more dynamic existing small businesses, of new companies left on the wayside by big corporations, of start-up concerns created by teams of experts and of the self-employed in virtually every area of human endeavour.

Such huge increases in subcontracting activities highlight the importance of considering all of the exchanges involved in the process of doing business, which in themselves are no more than the end results of the various collaborative processes inherent to every kind of business. Sales to end users of high-value-add products or services are preceded and succeeded by a range of dealings between various parties on both sides of a transaction. Customer purchasing agents do not necessarily actually themselves use the products they buy, and supplier sales representatives may know little about the actual manufacturing process or the details of the products and services they are selling.

Because the Internet lends itself so well to placing all forms of B2B dealings online, many companies, like IBM and ICE, prefer the term "e-business" to "e-commerce," maintaining the former is more comprehensive than the latter. E-business also takes into account all of the other exchanges that ultimately make commercial transactions possible. We totally endorse this point of view. Collaboration among all businesses will certainly contribute far more to the success of B2B e-commerce among small businesses than the technological ability of the latter to make or process payments online.

We hope this exploration of B2B e-commerce strategies will not only help shape the survival—but the boundless success—of small business heads and self-employed workers who choose to go this route over the next few years.

PART 1
TODAY

Chapter 1
The New Economy and Small Business

Small businesses and self-employed workers form the broad base of users targeted for business-to-business e-commerce (B2B) solutions. That is the main reason this revolutionary new way of doing business holds so much promise for these two groups.

To make the most of the new opportunities presented by B2B, these groups will have to take the initiative by mastering the rules of the New Economy and integrating them into their ways of doing business. If they succeed, the twenty-first century will be that of small, mobile organizations—or at least those best equipped to deal with the range of tools needed for working as teams over the Internet.

To assess the real benefits small business can reap from the Internet, we must begin by debunking the myth that it will hoist them to the ranks of the multinationals. This popular idea held a grain of truth at the start. But since the Internet has gone public, the investment, knowledge and luck needed to succeed means companies like Yahoo!, Amazon and Netgraphe are the exceptions, not the rule.

The new Linux operating system is a good example of how the New Economy has brought innovation to smaller organizations. Thanks to the Internet, Linux has emerged as a valid alternative to omnipresent MS Windows in less than a decade. The Internet enabled the collaboration of hundreds of programmers working together for free, in hopes of producing an operating system based on an open source code for all.

By mid-2000, as a result of this joint online effort, "Planet Linux" consisted of dozens of companies working exclusively in this field—plus some industrial giants contributing an increasing share of their resources and activities to the product. The collective energy resulting from this type of shared and pooled work, further fuelled by a real chance of making a profit, has become a source of concern for Microsoft.

Similar joint ventures could create upheavals in every sphere of economic activity. While not completely tilting the scales in favour of small business, B2B could certainly give it an edge. Knowledgeable small firms will be able to stand out by applying this new approach where short- and long-term partnerships or alliances—even between direct competitors—will serve as the foundations for flexible virtual enterprises, well positioned to respond to market conditions.

The evolution of e-commerce

When the Internet went commercial, numerous market gurus predicted the democratization of the digital economy through low cost direct access by small business. The Information Highway has substantially evolved since that time. We have witnessed the rise and fall of Netscape, the boom of companies like Yahoo! and Amazon.com, a market frenzy around such activities—followed by a collapse in resultantly inflated Internet share prices.

These developments substantially modified the stakes, in at least three respects:

- They accelerated technological development.
- They resulted in soaring costs for Web start-ups.
- They gave rise to a host of aggressive players in all market segments.

Naturally, such changes also hiked the ante for small businesses seeking to get involved in ecommerce. At the same time, they triggered a proliferation of technology and service providers, resulting in plunging softwaree prices. This made far more affordable a level of technical complexity and sophistication that had previously been the exclusive domain of only the biggest companies. Plus, small companies often have big cost advantages. With little in the way of existing computer equipment or technical experience, these enterprises can start from scratch—rather than having to establish costly bridges between their legacy systems and their new ecommerce applications.

Small business and e-commerce

This means the gurus' forecasts seem to be coming true in the case of B2B—while lagging with respect to retail e-commerce (e-tailing).

> Through trial and error, U.S. e-tailing started coming online in late 1998, but only within well-targeted niches. Because of its complexity and novelty, e-tailing seemed for a while to be re-served for new "dot-com" companies that came into being solely to profit from online sales. It was difficult to envision how typical small businesses could get established in areas where even huge retail chains were unable to deal with competition from upstarts ready to forfeit everything —including even minimal profits—for the sake of explosive growth.

> We have come to realize that large and well-established companies are not as poorly equipped as we may have imagined. Their abilities to simultaneously conduct sales over numerous channels have proven a huge advantage, if only in terms of marketing and the cost of getting new customers. Furthermore, e-tailing ventures are risky for small businesses lacking financial resources and technological savvy. Ultimately, e-tailing has become the exclusive preserve of companies that are either very big, or on their way to becoming so—at least in terms of the most popular products with nationwide distribution.

However, the B2B equation is quite different, for several reasons.

Although many businesses are right in saying they have no interest in e-tailing, not even the corner store falls outside the scope of B2B. Every business is part of a value-added chain that starts with the exploitation of natural resources and ends in our workplaces, in our homes and on our dinner plates[2].

Few companies are actually situated where the action is heaviest—in direct contact with individual consumers. However, all businesses, without exception, must deal with other companies or government agencies. Retail trade is just the tip of the iceberg, representing no more than 30% of the GDPs of industrialized nations. The biggest share of economic activity is increasingly found upstream, among knowledge-creation companies that generate either new information or information with added value.

Two factors have contributed to the rise in electronic exchanges of information. Users have achieved substantial productivity gains in terms of speed, decreased costs for both purchases and sales, elimination of paperwork and mistakes, closer teamwork with larger numbers of partners and so forth. In addition, service providers start earning big profits the moment they reach the break-even point, since the incremental costs of serving new users are lower once infrastructures have been amortized. Growing returns like these largely explain the big rush to provide B2B services of every kind that started during 1999 in the U.S.

Illustration 1   The Evolution of B2B

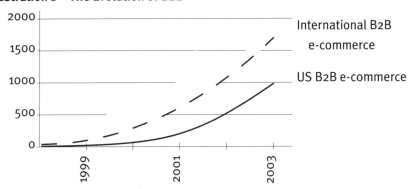

This is how Merril Lynch and Forrester foresee the B2B e-commerce evolution in the next three years (in $ billions U.S.)

2 See Chapter 2 Transforming the Value Chain.

The Sabre case is an excellent example of this phenomenon. This American Airlines-produced reservations system has substantially altered the ways travel agencies work. In so doing, it has managed to generate more profits for American Airlines than even the company's own ticket sales. In the U.S. healthcare industry, the ASAP (Analytic Systems Automatic Purchasing) system introduced in the 1970s by American Hospital Supply (AHS) has allowed hospitals to reduce the time needed to confirm orders from several days to ten seconds. It has simultaneously cut data input and inventory management costs by 80%. Furthermore, the benefits of electronic data interchange (EDI) for large companies and organizations have been amply demonstrated.

B2B will obviously contribute to the online migration of business relationships. It will also amplify many other trends that were initiated by new management techniques introduced before its advent. This is not just a matter of technology, but of mental attitudes. Methods of doing business will evolve to the point that they would have been unimaginable over the private and closed electronic networks that have so far served as cradles for B2B. We shall examine three aspects of this phenomenon that are likely to lock in these benefits for small business.

Table 1   Different approaches, different advantages

	EDI	Sabre	Internet
Electronic transactions	Yes	Yes	Yes
Aggregated information	No	Yes	Yes
Speedy installation	No	No	Yes
Low-cost access	No	No	Yes
Rich Media support	No	No	Yes
Open Marketplaces	No	Partially	Yes
Web of Marketplaces	No	No	Yes

Bear, Stearns & Co. Inc.

The pendulum swings in favour of buyers

So far, we have primarily described how the Internet is allowing small business to situate itself within existing EDI networks. These networks, however, are only used to provide a continuous supply of the goods and services that play a direct role in the value-added chain—meaning, the key ingredients involved in production. These constitute the smallest share of a company's purchases. Occasional and irregular purchases of goods and services involved in maintenance, repair and operations (MRO) often make up the lion's share of a company's expenditures. Purchases of information and communications technologies (ICT) software and equipment systems are, by themselves, responsible for the greatest share of current outlays for an increasing number of small businesses, including graphics studios, ad agencies, design firms, audiovisual producers and so forth.

The initial thrust of B2B on the Internet can moreover be largely explained by the efforts all industries have made to automate the procurement process. Naturally, such changes first took ICT purchases into account, as in the cases of Dell and Cisco. But they quickly caught on among suppliers of office equipment and a wide variety of service providers. The birth of vertical business communities, in which stock is auctioned off and services are bid at "reverse auctions," have helped B2B encroach on what was once the traditional sphere of EDI exchanges—continuous supply.

Both new and well-established firms—hoping to change the rules of the game as Sabre and ASAP have done in their respective fields—have invested in the various Web-based vertical markets for goods and services. Because they do not have to sell access to physical networks, such "electronic marketplaces" (or "e-marketplaces") are quickly asserting themselves on the Web. The heads of such enterprises are right in assuming they will be able to easily reach all of an industry's key players, because the pluses of being online are becoming increasingly critical to all businesses and organizations of any size.

In Chapter IV, we will cover the range of resources deployed by the e-business communities to attract buyers and sellers, but for the moment we shall start by mentioning that:

- These communities mainly benefit buyers, which include far more small businesses than large ones.

- Because of instantaneous electronic communications, they now far more efficiently reach the critical mass required for their deployment.

In the same way that e-tailing has reshuffled the deck to give individual consumers new resources at merchant expense, B2B will certainly provide a host of benefits for its most frequent users, small businesses and self-employed workers.

Virtual businesses

The Internet, however, opens much wider vistas. As the preferred means of rapid individual and group communications within closed or open-ended groups, it provides an amenable environment for a range of partnership projects that have become the daily fare of most businesses and organizations.

If we limit ourselves to transactional exchanges between separate companies, we deny ourselves the many other benefits of being online. As the development and proliferation of Linux technologies has clearly demonstrated, the Internet is the environment best suited for the emergence of virtual businesses, a concept popularized in the early 1990s and made possible by public digital networks.

With the wave of mega-mergers marking the transition to a new millennium, there is good reason to question how small business will contend with the emergence of the digital economy. In so doing, however, we might be overlooking the trend among large organizations to increasingly focus on core skills and outsource to specialized companies other functions that, while of increasing importance, remain accessory to their final goals. Along the lines of Nike and Ikea (but without employing their low-cost labour models), Cisco designs its own products and controls their distribution, while subcontracting all of their manufacturing.

This means small businesses could gain much power and influence in the digital economy. Thomas Malone, a professor at the Massachusetts Institute of Technology (MIT) and co-organizer of the work group called "Inventing the Organizations of the 21st Century," is a proponent of this idea.

> Prof. Malone notes how film production was long based on a concentration within the major studios of all the ingredients needed to make movies, including stars bound by exclusive contracts. The evolution of moviemaking, now based on the creativity and imagination of individual craftspersons —including crews that are put together at the start of each production and dismantled at the end—provides a foretaste of the new order that will prevail among a growing number of industries.

Even if we consider only the marketing function, we can see how rapid developments in business have resulted in the need for an increasing number of companies to ally themselves with creative studios to dress-up their products, boost the use of these products during appropriate events and make them known through the wide variety of available communications tools. In an era where students are sending prospective employers CD-ROM-based résumés, companies may find they need more than old-fashioned brochures to get their messages across.

Small is beautiful

Ultimately, the very size of a small business gives it a big edge in a world where the accelerating pace of business seems to be the only enduring constant. Not only are small businesses more flexible than bigger structures, they are often free from the handicap of legacy systems that must be imported into a new world. This means they can use their assets to more quickly adopt the latest innovations and initiate change in their respective fields. For small companies seeking to join the major leagues, mass customization and one-to-one marketing have become just as available as they are to big business.

As we can see, Internet-based B2B represents far more than a defensive strategy by which small businesses can keep key customers. This has, however, been the case with EDI, which small businesses adopted solely to comply with the demands of large buyers like Wal-Mart, Provigo and major car manufacturers.

If small businesses make the effort, they will be able to take advantage of new rules—already on their ways to becoming norms—to prosper. Self-employed workers and freelancers of all kinds will be the first to benefit. While we cannot guarantee that small business will prevail over multinationals, new ways of doing business will make it easier for them to play on level fields, through numerous and quickly restructurable joint ventures. Small businesses will gain greater autonomy and better control over their own destinies—rather than merely trailing in the wake of their respective sectors.

If you'd like to learn more...

Read the work of professors Thomas Malone and Michael Scott Morton, from the MIT Sloan School of Management, on Inventing the Organizations of the 21st Century.
http://ccs.mit.edu/21c/index.html

Check the unabridged version of the report Collective Reflection on the Changing Workplace, published in July 1997, by the Department of Labour in Ottawa.
http://www.reflexion.gc.ca/report_e.html

Read the study of Anne Troye-Walker, DG XIII analyst at the European Commission, Electronic Commerce: EU Policies and SMEs, pertaining to initiatives aimed at getting small businesses to adopt e-commerce.
http://europa.eu.int/ISPO/ecommerce/sme/reports/policies.html

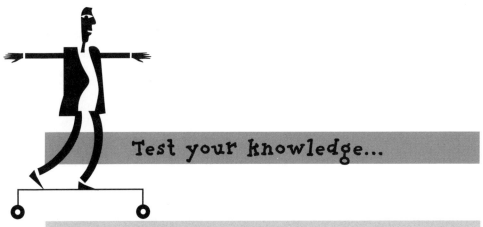

Test your knowledge...

Striking but little-known examples

Which Toronto company with 19,000 employees worldwide was able, thanks to collaborative commerce, to eliminate 80% of manufacturing defects and reduce from a week to one day the start of the production process? (Answer p. 188)

1. Celestica
2. Research in Motion
3. Softimage

Which California company, after only one year of collaborative commerce, was able to reduce its operating costs by $2,000,000, its production delays by 40%, and its inventory by 25%? (Answer p. 189)

1. Apple, Inc.
2. Adaptec
3. Universal Studios

In brief

- Small businesses and self-employed workers form the broad base of users targeted for business-to-business e-commerce (B2B) solutions.

- Short- and long-term partnerships or alliances—even between direct competitors—will serve as the foundations for flexible virtual enterprises, well positioned to respond to market conditions.

- Two factors have contributed to the rise in electronic exchanges of information: users have achieved substantial productivity gains and service providers start earning big profits the moment they reach the break-even point.

- We might be overlooking the trend among large organizations to increasingly focus on core skills and outsource to specialized companies other functions that, while of increasing importance, remain accessory to their final goals.

- Not only are small businesses more flexible than bigger structures, they are often free from the handicap of legacy systems that must be imported into a new world. This means such enterprises can use their assets to more quickly adopt the latest innovations and initiate change in their respective fields.

Chapter 2
Transforming the Value Chain

In collaboration with Renato Cudicio

For economists, the term "value chain" refers to the value added to a product at each stage of its production—from acquisition of raw materials through final sale. In traditional economics, this measurement corresponds to the quantity of physical work performed during each phase of the process. With the advent of the "information-based economy," added value becomes less a function of manual labour and more one of the "intelligence" with which a product is endowed. Knowledge is ultimately the essential ingredient in any intellectual work, including software, musical composition, professional training and accounting services.

Value can be added up or downstream in the production cycle without the need to reinvent basic products, often simply by providing a wider choice of options, sales information tailored to specific customer requirements or faster delivery to reduce inventory storage. Such new approaches to production management, known as "mass customization," "one-to-one marketing" and "just-in-time delivery," take on fresh significance when they go online. Far more effective because of fast communications, such differentiation strategies may at some point become universal among all businesses in the same fields, due to the use of open standards.

Until recently, B2B transactions were confined to a small number of companies. These firms had to be convinced to adopt technologies that were proprietary or relatively closed and expensive for small business. The Internet, however, has made trade possible among all suppliers, partners and customers in a given industry, as well as with the wide range of service providers and freelancers now found in the orbits of all private and public organizations.

Those companies most conversant with electronic interrelationships among all participants will be able to rise up the value chain, by continuing to build more "intelligent" features into their products and services. In this chapter, we shall consider how the Internet has affected changes in the value chain as a whole, along with its impact on supply, production and sales. Any one of these three functions can permit any company to redefine its place within the New Economy.

Information is a capital asset

Information has become vital to the production process for two main reasons:

- Opportunities to enhance the physical aspects of the manufacturing process are constantly shrinking, given the high levels of mechanization and automation already present in many industries. However, important gains in productivity may still be achieved through exchanges of information.

- The position of each player in the chain is a function of the value that player adds to the product. In B2B, inputs of information and intelligence should occur at all levels of the chain to improve the performance and effectiveness of all players in a particular industry.

Some years ago, knowledge management became the critical issue among leading-edge businesses. Performance in such companies depends on the ability to acquire a collective memory, unique know-how and a dynamic corporate culture, accompanied by many intangible assets that played a secondary role in the past. To succeed with this approach, an in-depth analysis is required of the ways in which information is obtained and exchanged not just within a company, but because of B2B, among its suppliers, partners and customers as well.

Changes of this kind in the value chain are not limited to hi-tech sectors. The enhanced standing of "information capital" has forced all companies to so evolve that divisions between traditional sectors of activity have become fuzzy. These kinds of developments are made possible by a basic reorientation of the Internet's role, as well as of information and communications technologies (ICT), in the production and distribution processes.

Design, production monitoring, ordering, billing, promotional literature and payment may now be done in real time over secure online tools. The management of inventory (or more properly, of its absence), just-in-time delivery (JIT), globalized procurement, and Web-based subcontracting or EDI, are applications that have naturally emerged from an integration of the Web into the business process.

In retail trade alone, the impact on relations between wholesalers and sales outlets will be huge, since online management applications have up until now been beyond the reach or budget of small business.

> In Quebec, for example, the central purchasing department of Marchands Unis provides small neighbourhood hardware stores with instant access to a catalogue of 30,000 products, enabling them to offer as much choice as mass merchandise outlets.

A new scale of values

Groundswells are currently rippling through the Quebec, Canadian and world economies. Forming the outlines of tomorrow's industry, these trends are not entirely new, but they will stun everyone by their scope. Companies seeking better positioning must adapt to the market structure not only of today, but of tomorrow. Because of the Internet, "tomorrow" means within as little as six months—and no more than one or two years.

A brief review of recent technological change will provide a better idea of the situation:

- In the 1970s, computerization served mainly to automate a variety of industrial and office routines, to facilitate mass production and to serve as a stimulus to progress in other human endeavours. However, the computer itself remained a highly technical and inaccessible tool. Information was exchanged on paper or at best through the operator of an interactive terminal linked to a mainframe—a process usually limited to large companies.

- From the early 1980s to the mid-1990s, information systems were marked by the proliferation of PCs and widespread use of office automation tools. This phenomenon resulted in widespread familiarity with computers by company employees. These computers started out as standalone equipment, not connected to networks. Data exchanges were made primarily by disk or on paper. Soon, however, Novell and private networks took over, although these systems were confined to the physical limits of a given organization.

- At the turn of the millennium, ICTs are establishing themselves within companies by optimizing the production and distribution processes to greatly improve the general quality of services offered. Such processes are no longer merely subject to internal overhaul, as was the case with the vast changes of the early 1990s, but to external transformations as well, since this is where most impediments to small business participation have so far resided.

Successful small businesses will participate in the value chain through increasingly complex and automated exchanges with big contract givers, other small businesses and specialists of every kind. By relying on their customers and the accumulated know-how of their respective industries, these enterprises will be able to complement their initial offerings with additional products and services from new partners to cover all the needs of these same customers, further boosting their loyalty and paving the way to an even larger number of accounts.

Illustration 2   Value chain evolution

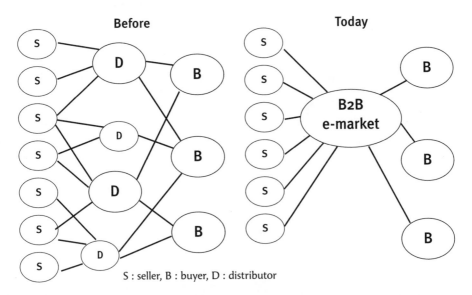

S : seller, B : buyer, D : distributor

In traditional commerce, the quasi totality of transactions go through one (or more) distributor, made indispensable by the lack of complete information on the market.

In the new model, an e-marketplace gives complete access to information to both buyer and seller, breaking the traditional distribution system.

Acquiring modern tools

Naturally, the more critical it becomes to obtain and communicate information, the more ICT needs will grow in business. B2B will become part and parcel of the ways companies do business. Small businesses will also be part of this trend and, because of their technological gap, analysts and suppliers now see them as the most active customers in the ICT industry.

> According to IBM, small business budgets for computer equipment and software climbed 12% in 1999, while those of large corporations—already far better equipped with such resources—rose a mere 9%. The processes of closely monitoring technological trends and of training employees accordingly—so

B2B applications can be profitably incorporated within existing systems—have become prerequisites not only for growth, but for maintaining credibility among customers.

The key technologies involved are:

- **Local and wide area networks** (intranets and extranets), have revolutionized this process by enabling email and e-commerce, telecommuting, work groups, voice and image communication and integrated management.

- Internal implementation of ERP, or Enterprise Resource Planning. By 2002, according to investment banking analysts Donaldson, Lufkin & Jenrette (DLJ), the installation of these systems should grow 15% or more annually, assuming the Application Service Provider (ASP) model proves valid[3]. SAP, Peoplesoft and Oracle offer these products to big business, while J.D. Edward does the same for smaller firms.

- **Monitoring tools**—these are generally Internet-based supply chain management resources for which DLJ predicts 32% growth by 2002, as they are perfectly suited to ERPs.

- **Customer relationship management applications** (CRM), commonly called front office solutions, should see growth of better than 29% by 2002 (also according to DLJ), by enhancing and accelerating the customer communications process.

- **Data mining** can look forward to a bright future, since real-time accessibility, analysis and storage of a wide range of data will henceforth be the key to most of these new applications.

- **Various e-commerce tools**, online procurement, virtual auctions, groupware, EDI transactions and so forth, are situated at the crossroads of these technologies and likely to permeate all aspects of the economy.

---

3 See Chapter V on outsourcing.

The new value chain

Numerous factors are thus involved in transforming the value chain, as its underlying exchanges gradually become distributed among various networks. The process began on private electronic networks. These electronic exchanges will progressively migrate to the universal network that is the Internet. As they do so, they will be quickly accompanied by the vast majority of transactions, still concluded offline. We shall see resulting impacts on small business relations among:

1. Suppliers (upstream)

2. Partners (in the middle)

3. Customers (downstream)

Procurement and e-marketplaces

While many small businesses adopted EDI technology to meet the demands of big customers, few did so to automate or synchronize their own procurement processes. Because they place relatively few orders, small businesses have largely ignored this system, principally due to its cost.

This cost barrier fell with the advent of the Internet. Small online businesses can actually bypass the EDI system to connect fairly easily to their main suppliers through simpler techniques, like Web forms, to both place and, in many cases, follow up on orders.

While this method does not give a small business the same level of automation as EDI affords large ones, it is much faster and cheaper than traditional phone or fax communications. That is why small businesses often use it to "get wet" in the interactive use of the Internet. This process is making the Internet a more effective channel of communications for business-to-business dealings.

Small businesses can also register with electronic e-marketplaces[4] that are trying to eliminate the "friction" intrinsic in the traditional value chain. These horizontal and vertical channels, which already overlap

4 See Chapter 9 Interactive Marketing.

all facets of American economic life, make Internet-based business-to-business communications a daily reality. In the mid-term, they will certainly be the cheapest and fastest routes to new suppliers.

Until now, small businesses rarely found it worth the effort to seek partners upstream through traditional channels like written calls to tender and attendance at trade shows. Before implementing such processes, a small business first needs to ensure that a resource to be contracted or a new production factor to be evaluated is of great strategic value.

Because of its ability to economically assemble a wide variety of information in one location, the Internet can organize large quantities of useful data about every kind of good or service. The Internet provides access to such data at costs far lower than the time and money it would take to achieve the same results through traditional means.

> Imagine being able to identify the five suppliers with the lowest prices that are most interested in winning order X for product or service Y, all on one Web site and often on the same day. Science fiction? Absolutely not. This is already a reality for hundreds of American self-employed workers and small businesses using this kind of reverse bidding system on BizBuyer.com or similar sites. They have the opportunity to compete with thousands of other suppliers of telephone systems, computer equipment, software, providers of specialized services (such as patent protection) and so forth.

Managers know from experience that the cost of buying a product or service should include the time spent selecting goods and communicating with the supplier, the time devoted to after-sales service and the time required for delivery. To limit the costs incurred by traditional methods, those in charge of procurement generally contact, at most, the five closest or best-known suppliers or distributors.

Given this situation, suppliers and distributors are at an advantage when buyers are not fully attuned to their markets. They can boost prices and benefit from what economists call a "monopoly rent." Even in the limited context of from "one to many," the increased access to Web-based horizontal and vertical business markets is quite likely to push prices downward, because buyers have become better informed.

At the same time, there is no reason why this system cannot evolve and transmit messages from "many to many."

> In the area of procurement, this will result in a flurry of purchasing cooperatives, which are much easier to set up on the Web than they are by mail or phone. In the area of e-tailing, the phenomenon already exists on the MobShop site where, the larger the number of consumers who band together and the greater their desire to buy, the lower they can push prices. The same system will certainly be carried over to business, where firms won't even have to team up to extract such benefits. Even in the absence of outside intermediaries, professional and industrial organizations will certainly take advantage of this opportunity and organize members who want to obtain the better buying power of a group purchase.

B2B is thus quite likely to cut procurement costs for small business. Even those small businesses unwilling to take risks in other areas requiring greater experience and investment will largely pay back their costs of hooking up to the Internet with side-benefits already available at the click of a mouse.

Production and partnerships

Email

Before even considering transaction-oriented applications, most new online business users will discover the magic of email, which lets them bypass packed agendas and overflowing voicemail systems. Email has already proved a boon within businesses, but can also extend to partnership networks outside companies. And email has made it increasingly difficult to distinguish between the respective contributions of full-time employees and outside partners to a given project.

Email is the first virtual activity to affect all industries, without exception. The most prosperous companies at the start of the twenty-first century will be those that have best integrated email management into their communications arsenals. In addition to being cheaper than phone or fax, email also considerably reduces the time it takes to complete a particular project. Many companies can work together on designing a product or service by almost instantly exchanging the results of their respective efforts. Files sent as email attachments can be modified as is. Less limited than paper-based or videotaped reports, virtual presentations can combine data, sounds and images to maximize impact or simply to reveal all aspects of a prototype.

This type of teamwork is already part of the way many small businesses operate. Companies located outside major hubs benefit most because, for example, the system lets them work more quickly with specialized creative or market research firms often located in urban areas. Email allows such firms to reduce the number of face-to-face meetings and boost the productivity of those that remain necessary.

Groupware

Email, as a standalone application, is chiefly suited to two-way relationships with occasional suppliers or for asynchronous follow-ups on relationships with regular partners. Email will eventually be supplemented by a new set of applications called "groupware," when the time comes to move on to the stage of working closely with various members of an internal team with one or more strategic partners. The necessary applications are hosted on a remote server protected by a firewall and can be password accessed by outside partners who thus form a "virtual work group"—possessing most of the advantages of a team set up in a single location.

> Groupware was pioneered by Lotus Notes, which is still the most widespread application of its type. Not far behind is Microsoft Exchange, trailed by Novell's GroupWise. All three can now run off the Web and can thus be mastered much more easily by small businesses starting from scratch.

There are many benefits to groupware. Since team members share a common "work space," they can more easily add files and more effectively share specialized and complementary skills. Groupware can be used for brainstorming sessions among remote participants or for group production of texts created through real-time or asynchronous exchanges. This system helps perpetuate the collective memory of a project, even when group membership changes over time, because of the simplicity with which its records can be checked. In this way a work history is always accessible, and previously issued expert opinions can be quickly retrieved when an earlier topic crops up again.

Internet

In addition to mainly asynchronous email and groupware functions, the Internet provides other tools that can be used when needed for intense simultaneous or real-time work sessions. Videoconferencing is quite likely to take off with the booming number of broadband-equipped small businesses, professional workers and independent creative experts. The minimal cost of equipment and software for such service is no longer an obstacle. Even instant messaging, a popular technology among young Web surfers for communicating with each other in real-time, is finding a place for itself in the business world, whenever an immediate response is required for a particular problem. Lotus SameTime, for example, runs behind firewalls and can encrypt communications, thus resolving security issues encountered with mass market systems like ICQ or AOL Messenger.

It is clear that the Internet will become the major platform for joint efforts among virtual businesses. There are many examples of companies that subcontract the manufacturing of their products not only to countries where labour is less expensive, but increasingly within their targeted markets, enabling them to optimize their supply chain logistics. Those involved in such processes are often linked by groupware like Notes. The simultaneous access Notes offers to a common information pool from any point of the globe also cuts down on a range of potential errors.

Sales and virtual globalization

As with all revolutions, B2B must endure its growing pains. While companies have every interest in becoming acquainted with its benefits so they can profit from its opportunities, they must also understand its risks so they can minimize any negative impact on sales. Companies should remember that supply-side benefits will be offset by problems with sales.

Much has been written and said about the almost magical effect of the Web for small businesses that manage to hoist themselves to the ranks of the multinationals through their Web sites and take on markets that had previously been beyond their reach. Conveyed by would-be gurus using sensational images for lack of better ideas, this myth unfortunately fails to deal with the difficulty of setting up effective sites and underestimates the flip side of the e-revolution—competition increases as companies penetrate new markets.

In addition to competition between the sites themselves, subcontractors in most industries will also compete on the vertical, horizontal or regional markets that have sprung up during our transition to a new millennium[5]. These new intermediaries will make the value chain more open in ways least desirable for suppliers. Concentrated on a single site, suppliers will be forced to adopt new rules of play that will be imposed throughout their respective industries.

> Certain analysts have played down the impact e-marketplaces might have on the continuous supply of raw materials and parts entering the production chain. Their argument is based on the fact that order givers have already achieved maximum possible savings by reducing the numbers of suppliers they use or by selecting suppliers from countries with cheaper labour.
>
> Despite the short history of e-marketplaces, we already know this is not so. Just on the manufactured parts markets—estimated at some $5 billion U.S. in the United States—numerous big companies like GM, United Technologies and Raytheon saw

5 See Chapter IV.

their supply costs drop an average 15%, as written calls for tenders began appearing on the FreeMarkets Web auction site.

Much impressed by such results, GM executives decided to set up their own vertical e-marketplace in conjunction with new B2B player CommerceOne. They later merged their e-marketplace with its Ford counterpart, co-designed with Oracle. Called Covisint, this automobile industry marketplace was immediately endorsed by Daimler/Chrysler and Renault/Nissan, making it a must for industry subcontractors.

The existence of such e-marketplaces could eventually trigger ongoing price wars between subcontractors on a wide range of parts and components. Because supplier lists can be redrawn almost instantaneously, order givers may be tempted to review special or well-established relationships with some subcontractors when they believe it is in their interests to do so.

Such changes, however, will have positive effects on top-performing companies better able to expand their potential customer pools by building on their e-marketplace experiences. The remainder will only manage to stay in the race by benefiting from other B2B benefits involving procurement or the subcontracting of non-core activities, so they can achieve the kind of competitiveness they need to break even in the e-marketplaces.

If you'd like to learn more...

Read Exploiting the Virtual Value Chain by Jeffrey Rayport and John Sviokla, from the Harvard Business School, appearing on the site of the McKinsey management consulting firm.
http://www.mckinseyquarterly.comarticle_page.asp?articlenum=132

Read the article by Andreas Zielke and Mathias Pohl "Virtual Vertical Integration: The Key to Success," in The McKinsey Quarterly, focusing on differentiation factors in the equipment manufacturing sector.
http://www.mckinseyquarterly.com/article_page.asp?articlenum=178

Read 4 Questions for the ACID Information AGE, an essay by John Sviokla, a former Harvard professor who became a partner at Diamond Technology Partners, published on the site Manufacturing.Net, a co-venture of Cahners Business Information and i2 Technologies, an expert in automation of the logistics chain.
http://www.manufacturing.net/scl/scmr/4questions/4questions.htm

In brief

- With the advent of the "information-based economy," added value becomes less a function of manual labour and more one of the "intelligence" with which a product is endowed.

- Those companies most conversant with electronic interrelationships among all participants will be able to rise up the value chain, by continuing to build more "intelligent" features into their products and services.

- Successful small businesses will participate in the value chain through increasingly complex and automated exchanges with big contract givers, other small businesses and specialists of every kind.

- Because of its ability to economically assemble a wide variety of information in one location, the Internet can organize large quantities of useful data about every kind of good or service.

- B2B is thus quite likely to cut procurement costs for small business.

- Email allows firms to reduce the number of face-to-face meetings and boost the productivity of those that remain necessary.

- There are many benefits to groupware: team members share a common "work space," they can more easily add files and more effectively share specialized and complementary skills. Groupware can be used for brainstorming sessions among remote participants or for group production of texts created through real-time or asynchronous exchanges. This system helps perpetuate the collective memory of a project, etc.

- Because supplier lists can be redrawn almost instantaneously, order givers may be tempted to review special or well-established relationships with some subcontractors when they believe it is in their interests to do so.

CHAPTER 3
SALES OUTLETS ON THE WEB

The Internet has given rise to as many ways and means of selling as exist in the real world. And, like the latter, a company's B2B activities can take many directions at once. The various channels it ultimately selects may reinforce each other or stand completely apart, resulting in a wide range of strategic choices with entirely different results. Each company must set its own course, channel by channel, based on available budget and technological sophistication in the targeted sector. The possibility also arises of strategic hybrids that combine virtual sales channels with traditional physical ones, known as "clicks and bricks" businesses.

The various sales channels discussed below have existed since the start of Internet-based B2B. They include direct sales from Web sites, Internet-based digital document (EDI) exchanges, e-marketplaces and auction sites. Other channels will probably appear and some will merge, as has already occurred in some auction e-marketplaces. In this chapter, we shall consider the different approaches from the perspective of sales as well as explore their prospective benefits.

While B2B shares common features with e-tailing, it also remains accessible to a wide range of other innovations because the Internet opens the door to once unimaginable initiatives now deployable with unprecedented swiftness. The resulting boom in B2B at the start of the twenty-first century means strategic issues must be well thought out. What had once been "cast-in-stone" business models are likely to be of little value for at least the first five years of this decade—and may even vanish for good. This is one of the first ways e-business has affected the ways things were once done in the traditional economy.

Illustration 3   From EDI to B2B

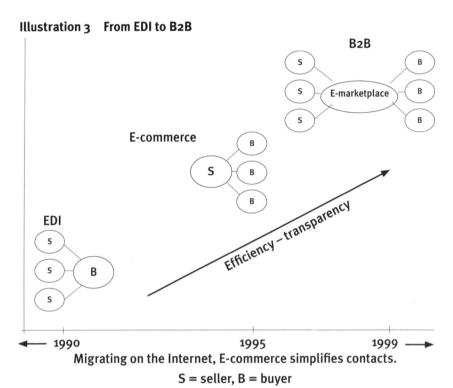

Migrating on the Internet, E-commerce simplifies contacts.

S = seller, B = buyer

Inspired by Morgan Stanley Dean Witter, Collaborative commerce, *April 2000.*

Direct sales from Web sites

From the start, Web sites—the Internet's best-known attraction—have promised solutions ranging from cures for every ill to the simple business card. Companies lacking Web sites are perceived as being outside the loop. Conversely, the often-repeated maxim that Web sites will allow any company to play on a level field with the multinationals in cyberspace is not necessarily true. Web sites can, however, support and maintain company sales in many ways.

Even more important than its direct contribution to a company's financial results, a Web site is a marketing and after-sales service tool[6].

6 These features will be further discussed in Chapter 9: Interactive Marketing.

Tricks and tips

Beyond providing basic information on products and services, Web sites must be user friendly, offering visitors a maximum of opportunities to learn more and to get in touch with human representatives. Relationships created in this manner can be maintained in B2B, even at a distance. A toll-free number, addresses of the head office and regional outlets, along with local phone numbers, names of suppliers, names of customer-relations managers (for each product and region), their email addresses, names of key partners and associates and requests for comments or suggestions, are just a few ideas for turning mere visitors into future customers or partners.

Electronic order forms

Many sites initiate the sales process with electronic order forms (or "shopping carts") that calculate the cost of products and services selected—once their features, quantities, delivery deadlines and so forth have been specified. The corresponding price can be instantly furnished when the information entered by the customer constitutes a standard order. In the case of unusual or custom orders, prices can be promply provided by email.

Online ordering

The next phase involves online ordering, which may be easily accomplished using an HTML-based form. This process is simple and well suited to companies expecting relatively few Internet-based sales, either because these will represent only a small portion of total sales or because they are only being tested on an experimental basis.

If a company hopes to maximize Web-based sales and earn significant revenues online, various Internet-based applications must be integrated into existing or future management systems. This is a difficult task, because it means reviewing business procedures and setting up "middle-ware" to harmonize and integrate a company's various applications.

Electronic catalogues

The most sophisticated companies will want to set up electronic cata-logues for their products and tailor these catalogues to specific accounts. This will enable repeat customers viewing the catalogues to place their usual orders and obtain specific price lists integrating discounts accord-ing to purchasing volumes.

Payment

Payment for most B2B transactions will be offline, until such time e-payment and authorization methods become more widespread. But this will come to pass. Because of higher values on most orders, business-to-business exchanges are less suited than e-tailing transactions for credit card purchases, by far the most common means of Internet-based payment.

EDI over the Internet

Electronic document interchange (EDI[7]) accounted for some 80% of business-to-business transactions at the start of the new millennium. Since the 1970s, the application of its various standards for transmitting purchase orders, bills, waybills, transfers of funds and so forth, has gradually increased, especially in the retail distribution, car, electronic

---

7 See Chapter 6 for more detail.

component and aerospace sectors where big order givers have attempted to convert all of their regular suppliers to this system.

EDI's advantages

EDI offers many advantages to big business, including elimination of paperwork, fewer mistakes and a faster flow of information. EDI applications were designed to use asynchronous computer-to-computer communications over private and proprietary networks and are thus fairly difficult to connect to existing management systems. Their prime function is to handle recurring purchases, including those directly involved in the value chain. These might be parts for a car maker, or food products for a supermarket chain.

The evolution of EDI

Lacking adequate trade volume to benefit from this system themselves, small businesses acquainted with EDI use it in one direction only—for exchanges with their main customers. Until very recently, such exchanges took place over specialized, private "value-added networks" (VAN), which serve as hubs between suppliers and big order givers. The best-known VANs in North America are GE Information Services, Sterling Commerce and Harbinger.

Because quite a few businesses refused to adopt EDI after deciding it was not worth the investment, the big EDI order givers were able to convert no more than 80% of their suppliers to this electronic transaction system. As long as old-fashioned paper swaps remain at least partly necessary, full EDI benefits will not be realized.

Since the Internet is much cheaper than VANs—which require fairly high software installation costs for small businesses, accompanied by recurring transmission fees—e-commerce experts considered the Internet, from the outset, an ideal means of connecting small business holdouts to the EDI applications of big companies. Web/EDI forms, accessible from the site of a VAN or even that of an order giver, can thus be used to convey information as if it were actually being sent through the EDI system.

More sophisticated EDI software has also been designed to let small businesses transact among themselves, as well as comply with the procedures of major accounts. A new technologically oriented Quebec firm, Dynec, has taken on this market by developing kits adapted to the EDI procedures of major food chains.

E-marketplaces

Whatever the total volume of B2B transactions processed through e-marketplaces[8], it is clear these forums will change the rules of supply for all industries. Even if they have a direct impact on no more than 20% of B2B exchanges by 2003, it is quite likely, according to the conservative predictions of the Volpe Brown investment bank, that price levels negotiated in these public marketplaces will also affect buyer-supplier prices.

Illustration 4   The seller in B2B

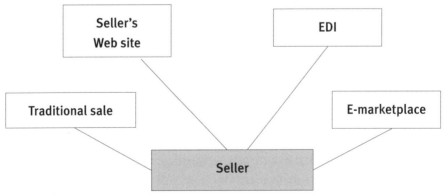

B2B e-commerce multiplies the number of selling channels the seller can acess.

---

8 See Chapter 4 Business Communities.

The advantages of e-marketplaces

Small businesses will find it in their interests to join one or more e-marketplaces, if only to keep tabs on their respective industries. In the United States, more than twenty such markets existed for the chemical industry in the spring of 2000. Some thirty were present in the even more fragmented construction industry. At least one American e-marketplace is present in virtually every area of human endeavour, ranging from healthcare to funeral services.

> Covisint, certainly the best-known e-marketplace, is a vertical portal for the "Big Three" American car manufacturers and the Federal Trade Association has scrutinized its operations to make sure it is not in violation of the Antitrust Act. The Worldwide Retail Exchange, a consortium formed by more than twenty major American and European retailers, including Kmart and the Gap, in the United States, and Auchan and Casino, in France, has also been the focus of attention after awarding a record B2B contract to Ariba, IBM and i2 Technologies. Of the twenty American e-marketplaces specifically focusing on small business needs, Onvia—a Canadian start-up—managed to register a half million users by the spring of 2000, just two years after the launch of its U.S.-based site.

In the case of companies that know little about e-commerce, e-marketplaces offer sales opportunities unhindered by the technical complications inherent in construction of a Web site. Out of a concern for boosting visits to their sites, operators of these marketplaces often make deals with suppliers to draw buyers. Fees for billable services (on top of the commissions charged by most e-marketplaces) are only applied once buyers have achieved a clearly critical mass for the seller.

Notwithstanding the long-term price pressures on all suppliers, which are likely to change the rules of the game in every industry[9], American e-marketplaces are clearly offering new export channels for Canadian and Quebec small businesses that continue to benefit from a favourable exchange rate, whether or not these companies already maintain U.S.

9 See Chapter 2 Transforming the Value Chain.

presences. Those with the courage to barge into the U.S. market can kill two birds with one stone by increasing the number of their sales outlets as they learn new ways of doing business—ways certain to gradually spread throughout Canada.

E-marketplaces and Web sites

The proliferation of e-marketplaces in the United States has led many observers to question the need for companies to continue maintaining their own Web sites. But while these marketplaces are excellent ways for companies to test the waters of e-commerce, they cannot meet all needs. For companies trying to explore all the different ways of selling their goods, a Web site is a particularly useful vertical platform for communicating with steady customers and for supplying them at lower cost by cutting out e-marketplace fees.

New marketplaces

The changes e-marketplaces will bring to relations between suppliers and buyers are still unclear. At this early point in their history, it is difficult to predict whether the standards of neutral intermediaries or those of the biggest players in each industry will ultimately prevail. But one thing is certain. Because of their "many to many" communications models, these multilateral trading posts will not just stay with us, they will have a big impact on the evolution of B2B—particularly in the case of small business.

Auction sites

Online auctions for businesses have become so popular that some observers have dared to predict the almost universal rule of prices set in advance will soon be a thing of the past. While this prediction may not be entirely true, it is clear that income generated from the sale of new and used goods or services will become increasingly common as online auctions gain in importance.

E-tailing auctions

Online auctions are big business in the e-tailing community. Thanks to eBay, business dealings that were once of marginal importance—and considered by the general public to be confined to flea markets and garage sales—have been pushed to the fore. Collectors of all sorts are no longer isolated and can be found every day in communities with thousands of members. Such numbers mean the more enterprising are now able to turn what had been hobbies into full-time occupations.

B2B auctions

The Internet has had an equally immediate impact within the electronics industry in the case of B2B transactions, for one clear reason. This is a sector in which outdated stock abounds, due to the rapid evolution of technology.

Inventory management

Auctions of electronic components and specialized chips have enabled manufacturers and distributors to find buyers interested in getting good prices for brand new but technologically outmoded products. Technologies Interactives Mediagrif, set up on the South Shore of Montreal, has created four auction sites targeted to this specific need—Broker Forum, Virtual Chip Exchange, Memory Network and PowerSource Online.

> Point2.com is a Western Canadian success story, this one involving the market for used heavy equipment. This equipment is often in very good condition and frequently becomes available when a big contract comes to an end or when natural resource extraction operations shut down. After getting financial backing

from Toronto's Bid.com public auction site, Point2.com took off as one of the North American leaders in its sector.

Many industries are burdened by stock that cannot be sold for a variety of reasons. In the case of plastics and chemicals, an estimated 15% of production fails to meet customer quality standards. Almost all manufacturing sectors end up with unsold inventory because of typical delays in reacting to decreasing demand.

In the past, excess stock and outdated or defective goods were sent off to liquidators, recycled or merely tossed in the trash. With liquidators, manufacturers only recovered up to 10% of the top market values of their goods.

Variable prices and returns

At online auction sites, with far more potential buyers, these products can easily be sold for top dollar. The Internet has thus proved quite useful in boosting the performance of companies that not long ago had to assume dead losses on part of their stock.

The ability of the Internet to bring buyers and sellers to a single location bears minuses as well as pluses. Vertical e-marketplaces are also subject to another type of auction that tends to cut into the earnings of sellers, who are placed in competition with each other by buyers who send out calls to tender to meet current supply needs. As we saw in Chapter II, FreeMarkets made such systems its specialty. It is more than likely that most vertical e-marketplaces will also host such auctions over the long run.

While the fixed price rule might be replaced by one of dynamically adjusted prices, the impact on it will probably be most strongly felt through "reverse auctions." This approach assumes that a buyer will select a short list of qualified suppliers, to obtain the lowest price for fulfilling a specific order. While this system is not much different from the usual tendering procedure that follows a contract's expiration, it will be much more widespread over the Internet because it offers a larger number of potential suppliers. Moreover, because it is so easy to institute, it can be used far more often.

Illustration 5 Dynamic prices

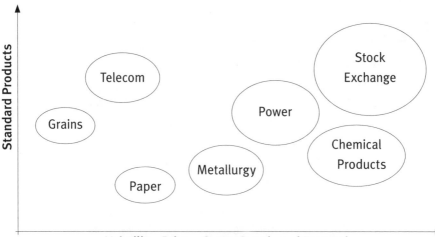

Volatility: Prices, Costs, Supply and Demand
Morgan Stanley Dean Witter, Collaborative Commerce, *April 2000*

To date, the Internet has provided that environment closest to the perfect conditions of a free market—a space in which both buyers and sellers have equal knowledge of supply and demand. As such, some economists have concluded that it will lead to the "frictionless economy" envisioned by Adam Smith. But even if it does not manage to do so, the New Economy will at the very least provoke far greater price fluctuations in a large number of industrial and commercial sectors.

If you'd like to learn more...

Read Make Your Site Sell, a site maintained in Hudson, Quebec, by Ken Evoy, a former McGill University professor turned Internet sales specialist. This site distributes his intellectual works, including his book of the same name—considered by many experts the best of its type. The site also contains a host of information useful for newcomers to the field. http://myss.sitesell.com/

Read "Speculative Microeconomics for Tomorrow's Economy," an article by J. Bradford DeLong and A. Michael Froomkin, the former a professor of economics at the University of California at Berkeley and the latter a professor of law at the University of Miami. This essay explores the impact of the Internet on the market economy, focusing on the role of online auctions. http://firstmonday.org/issues/issue5_2/delong/index.html

Read "New World Economic Order," an article by Ephraim Schwartz, Dan Neel and Eugene Grygo, in InfoWorld, concerning the benefits of online auctions for small businesses. http://www.infoworld.com/articles/hn/xml/00/07/17/000717hnbig2small.xml

In brief

- A Web site is a marketing and after-sales service tool.

- Online ordering is simple and well suited to companies expecting relatively few Internet-based sales.

- Repeat customers may use online catalogues to place their usual orders and obtain specific price lists integrating discounts according to purchasing volumes.

- Payment for most B2B transactions will be offline.

- EDI offers many advantages to big business, including elimination of paperwork, fewer mistakes and a faster flow of information.

- Small businesses will find it in their interests to join one or more e-marketplaces, if only to keep tabs on their respective industries.

CHAPTER 4
E-MARKETPLACES AS FAR AS THE EYE CAN SEE

The proliferation of vertical, horizontal, and geographic e-marketplaces is one of the most interesting developments in Internet-based e-commerce. B2B e-marketplaces are online meeting places where visitors can find information, suppliers, partners and even clients—and they are prospering. B2B has become the new frontier in electronic commerce for venture capital firms.

B2B e-marketplaces all aim at reformulating dealings between buyers and suppliers to optimize the value-added chain, from raw materials to finished products. The same method that enabled major corporations to successfully streamline their operations in the nineties is being applied to exchanges among businesses.

While threatening the very existence of distributors, wholesalers and brokers, the Internet has also breathed new life into the functions of these intermediaries by challenging, thanks to the proliferation of e-marketplaces, the unnecessary processes found in nearly every industry.

This very clear business model was, nonetheless, rocked to the core by the collapse of Internet stocks in the spring of 2000. Many independent start-up e-marketplaces were forced to postpone their stock exchange listings or merge with one another. Others have forged alliances with established virtual business marketplaces that act as buyers' or sellers' groups within a particular industry.

The phenomenon has a good chance of making itself a fixture in the e-commerce landscape, despite the bumpy road. The stock market's problems have actually had a positive impact outside the U.S. Local contenders have been given a chance to occupy their markets before the Americans come onto the scene.

Figure 6   Growth of cybermarkets

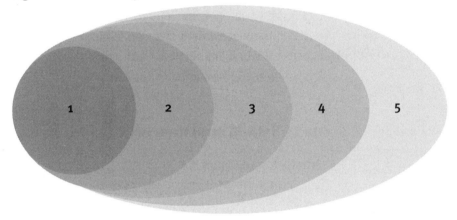

1. Order Matching
2. One-to-One Marketing
3. Content Aggregation
4. Fulfillment
5. Demand and Supply Chain Collaborations

Morgan Stanley Dean Witter, Collaborative Commerce, *April 2000*

Profitable communities

Many academicians have underscored the value of these forums to buyers and sellers. John Hagel, a consultant at McKinsey, recently popularized the concept of the "infomediary" in his books Net Gain and Net Worth. He explains the role of the infomediary is not simply to transmit products and services to buyers, but to play a more detailed role in supply, sub-contracting, cooperation and other areas. Unlike the traditional wholesaler, infomediaries do not necessarily handle merchandise per se. Rather, they try to facilitate the exchange of information between parties to a transaction.

Most such business portals deal with vertical markets, although a few respond to horizontal demand like the supply of office-related goods. Some e-marketplaces are geographically oriented, with the aim of reinforcing a particular region's competitiveness. Many American e-marketplaces aim to serve the specific needs of small business.

The Gartner Groups estimated there were some five hundred e-marketplaces operating in late 1999. In a subsequent study, they calculated that earnings of such enterprises were up 171% for that year, soaring from $183 million U.S. to $500 million U.S. The Volpe Brown Whelan investment bank estimates transactions originating from these business communities will make up 20% of all ecommerce exchanges in 2002. Forrester Research predicts th e proportion will rise to 54% in 2004.

The first business communities were developed for the electronics industry, closely followed by the chemical products industry with players such as Chemdex, PetroChemNet, ChemConnect, CheMatch, and SciQuest.com. Some dozen contenders have taken on the metallurgy market, the most senior being MetalSite and eSteel.

Seeking to apply its expertise to the broadest number of vertical markets, VerticalNet grouped together fifty-seven e-marketplaces in the early fall of 2000, including Chemical Online and four forums dealing with specialized metallurgical fields. Under its new name of Ventro, Chemdex applied the same logic when it diversified into related sectors with three new e-marketplaces. Another grouping of vertical markets was set up by Industrytoindustry.com (i2i). Launched in 1999 at the World Economic Forum under its founding president, Klaus Schwab, i2i is active in the United States, Europe, and Asia.

Large buyers step into the field

Flush with venture capital, the mushrooming marketplaces quickly invaded traditional industries in the U.S. Net Market Makers' agri-food directory listed fifty-two e-marketplaces in August 2000—about twenty more such forums than were present in the computer and telecommunications industries. In the construction business, an industry perfectly suited to the concept because of its extensive fragmentation, twenty-four e-marketplaces were in existence.

The entire game changed in the first quarter of 2000. Large multinationals entered the field with the goal of controlling the dominant e-marketplaces in their respective industries. One after the other, combined marketplaces were launched by giants in the automobile, aviation, food and clothing industries, each hoping for a success similar to that of American Airlines with its Sabre system—before an Internet-based concern could beat them to the punch.

Regulation

It is still too early to determine if the market will settle in with neutral marketplaces operated by independent players—or prefer marketplaces controlled by dominant players in an industry. The enthusiasm of these large players for the Internet has attracted the scrutiny of American and European regulators who are reviewing the intentions of some e-marketplace backers. To win a green light to proceed, these backers must demonstrate contract givers cannot use such forums to collude and, in so doing, force supplier prices down.

Is EDI fading away?

It is certain the deployment of e-marketplaces by large buyers will result in a faster move of EDI transactions to the Internet. The biggest users of EDI, including the automotive and retail distribution industries, were among the first to place a premium on this new method of procurement. We expect EDI technology to fade into the background, and small businesses, simply able to connect to e-marketplaces over their Web browsers, will no longer be forced to use EDI to conduct business with big contract givers. The EDI standard will, however, still govern communications between e-marketplaces and large contract givers, little disposed to drop a system in which they have invested so heavily.

Room to breathe outside the U.S.

While competition from e-marketplace syndicates had little impact on their independent counterparts in the fall of 2000, shrinking financial markets have reduced tech stock prices across the board, already forcing many independent e-marketplaces to modify their business plans. For example:

- Agri-food industry independents have merged.

- Ventro now offers tech support to e-marketplace members.

- Many marketplaces have adopted the application service provider formula[10].

- Some independent e-marketplaces have teamed up with e-marketplace syndicates.

For local players outside the U.S., the problems in the American marketplaces have been like a breath of fresh air.

Quebec

QuebecTel's electronic marketplace at www.Bizznys.com is aimed at small business and self-employed workers. A joint venture of Rona and Mediagrif Interactive Technologies, www.VRMO.com provides B2B maintenance, repair, and operations (MRO) services. Three virtual business communities were planned for late 2000. They are www.trousseca.com offering accounting services, www.agroclic.com aimed at the agri-food industry, and one tentatively named NetMetal for the metallurgical industry. These three communities result from

---

10 See Chapter V.

research by the Centre francophone d'informatisation des organisations, with support from the Quebec government's Information Highway fund—Fonds de l'autoroute de l'information.

Canada

A major Canada-wide project, www.Procuron.com, will benefit from BCE Emergis's partnership with Bell Canada and three large banks to combine their procurement needs. The service will be offered to all companies and will enjoy a very large volume of exchanges from the start.

After the involvement of venture capital concerns and major order givers, the third most important factor in the current boom is the rivalry from technology suppliers aiming to put together e-marketplace structures. Two mega-mergers and two major communications and information technology companies are currently engaged in a pitched battle for this exploding market.

The technical anchors for the concept are Ariba and CommerceOne. These two computer firms specialize in the development of Internet procurement systems for large companies. Ariba teams with IBM and i2 Technologies, the leader in supply chain management systems. CommerceOne partners with GE, as well as with SAP, a leader in integrated management systems. Oracle plans to become a main supplier of e-marketplace technology on its own, while Microsoft, hoping to benefit from the ubiquity of its software among small businesses, is offering its tools to link corporate databases with e-marketplaces through its E-business Acceleration Initiative (EBAI), unveiled in November 2000.

Winning conditions

E-marketplaces exist primarily to bring together a large number of suppliers for the same product. In the "real" world, buyers search for suppliers by phone and fax and get bids from up to five prospects. But with electronic business communities, companies can locate hundreds of sellers instantly. Most e-marketplaces operate on the reverse-auction principle that lets a buyer almost instantly target the lowest tender, eliminating the need to contact individual suppliers one by one.

Tricks and tips

Many factors combine to make e-marketplaces a success. The Bear Sterns investment bank lists the following six:

- A large volume of business. Industries with a multitude of transactions are ideal candidates. The retail sales sector with its recurring orders among many suppliers is a perfect example.

- A large number of suppliers and buyers. Highly fragmented industries such as the chemical sector are good targets for e-marketplaces. Consulting online databases using a search function is much easier than endlessly leafing through printed catalogues.

- Strong similarities between suppliers. The ease of comparing price, availability, after-sales service, and delivery deadlines of packing material over the Internet is a good example.

- The high cost of seeking information. Purchasers in industries whose products have short shelf lives, such as electronic parts, can get a better picture of a tender offer because prices are quickly updated and changes in inventories can be tracked easily over the Internet.

- The high cost of comparing products. In the case of products that are indistinguishable from one supplier to the next, such as foodstuffs, a Web page that clearly compares characteristics, available quantities, delivery delays, etc., eliminates the need for a buyer to produce a comparison chart.

- High expense of the procurement process. Approval procedures, credit checks, and order tracking all increase the cost of
  procurement. Most of these operations can be automated in
  a e-marketplace.

An important facet of any business community is the level of confidence
buyers place in the community's promoters and vendors. Promoters are
expected to remain neutral, not favouring one supplier over another.
Vendors are naturally expected to deliver on their commitments to
supply and to provide excellent after-sales service.

> MetalSite counts three major metal industry suppliers among its
> financial backers. To dispel any scepticism this situation could
> produce, MetalSite has assigned Andersen Consulting to regu-
> larly investigate the site's integrity and thereby reassure buyers.

To ensure their reliability, business communities independently and
regularly check the truthfulness of information supplied by their vendors. Many also offer purchaser ratings and opinions on vendors.

Guaranteed benefits for buyers

E-marketplace serve mainly to improve business practices in a given
industry. They achieve this goal by, for example, reducing transaction
costs, providing clear product comparisons and providing access to a
large number of vendors.

Naturally, these benefits are primarily to buyers. Vendors, on the other
hand, take advantage of the increased exposure and can save on reduced
transaction costs.

Sellers, however, may occasionally receive the most tangible benefits.
With access to a large number of potential buyers, they can auction
off what would otherwise be stock that is unsellable—or sellable only
at lower prices.

With the proliferation of U.S.-based e-marketplaces, the most pes-
simistic analysts predict consolidation will reduce their number to some
fifty by the year 2001. Successful e-marketplaces will have to integrate

new for-fee services, such as extending operational logistics to the entire value chain. Original business plans, usually constructed around the concept of small transaction fees, will not suffice to guarantee a e-marketplace's viability.

Business-to-business communities will gradually integrate themselves into the marketing practices of most companies. Virtual business communities will probably end up replacing the spot markets now provided by trade shows. In the same way that the Internet has encouraged a rebirth of written correspondence between individuals (but in a new form), it has breathed new life into the public marketplace, reborn as the e-marketplace.

Table 2   E-marketplace advantages

	For buyers	**For sellers**
Market	Easier to find new products, to discover new sellers	Increase in the number of new buyers
Price	Price transparency	Price pressure, but lower marketing costs
Transaction	Lower transaction costs	Lower transaction costs

If you'd like to learn more...

Visit the site of NMM (Net Market Makers), a private research firm, set up in 1998 to monitor the B2B e-commerce market. The company was bought out in the summer of 2000 by Jupiter Communications. http://www.nmm.com/

Visit Net Market Builders, a site dedicated to B2B e-commerce, set up by a team of consultants who claim to have helped found a number of major e-marketplaces. http://www.netmarketbuilders.com/

Read The B2B Analyst, a B2B newsletter published weekly by Jon Ekoniak and Tim Klein, analysts for real-estate brokers U.S. Bancorp Piper Jaffrey. http://www.nmm.com/documents/B2B_Analyst.htm

Visit http://www.b2business.net/Cool/
This site provides a wide range of resources, including numerous links to information on e-marketplaces.

In brief

- Unlike the traditional wholesaler, infomediaries do not necessarily handle merchandise per se. Rather, they try to facilitate the exchange of information between parties to a transaction.

- It is certain the deployment of e-marketplaces by large buyers will result in a faster move of EDI transactions to the Internet.

- Shrinking financial markets have reduced tech stock prices across the board, already forcing many independent e-marketplaces to modify their business plans.

- E-marketplace serve mainly to improve business practices in a given industry. They achieve this goal by, for example, reducing transaction costs, providing clear product comparisons and providing access to a large number of vendors.

- Vendors, on the other hand, take advantage of the increased exposure and can save on reduced transaction costs.

- Business-to-business communities will gradually integrate themselves into the marketing practices of most companies. Virtual business communities will probably end up replacing the spot markets now provided by trade shows. In the same way that the Internet has encouraged a rebirth of written correspondence between individuals (but in a new form), it has breathed new life into the public marketplace, reborn as the e-marketplace.

Chapter 5
Internet-Enabled Outsourcing

A new category of IT services, the Application Service Provider (ASP) model, first emerged in mid-1998 with the main goal of speeding small business's adoption of B2B ecommerce by 2005.

Second-generation ASPs have taken on the roles of service bureaus that remotely process payrolls of big businesses, with mainframe computers still out of the financial reach of most. Nowadays, ASPs want to use the Internet to help small businesses:

- Set up software applications

- Support and manage such applications

- Secure their transactional systems

- Acquire certain skilled services (and cut down on recruitment costs)

If this approach manages to overcome the issues that have stunted the growth of ASPs to date, it will certainly appeal to many businesses. The ASP model offers partial or complete remote information management services to end users. In its purest form, the customer owns no software applications and uses the ASP application-hosting infrastructure on a pay-as-you-go basis.

ASPs provide various end user services such as software set-up, hosting and management, and can ultimately lease software accessible to users over the Internet or any private network. Traditional outsourcing firms, on the other hand, limit their activities to on-site management of customer systems. And, while ASPs do provide Web hosting services similar to those offered by most ISPs, they distinguish themselves from the latter by assisting in the management of an organization's internal and external communications systems.

Just like most Internet-based business models, the ASP market was established by start-up concerns, but was quickly invaded by traditional outsourcing firms and ISPs that considered this new territory an extension of their current range of offerings. The ASP market is now fast gaining momentum, fuelled by the involvement of the entire computer industry. All of the players, from hardware and software manufacturers to consultants and systems integrators, are frantically adapting products and services to an ASP model, if they do not operate one themselves.

Step-by-step adoption plan

Industry analyst group IDC singles out six main categories of applications available through the ASP delivery model:

- Analytical: financial, customer turnover, site hits, etc.

- Vertical: manufacturing production planning, healthcare billing, insurance claims, etc.

- Management: human resources, accounting, inventory, procurement, etc.

- Marketing: sales force, customer service, etc.

- Collaborative: groupware, email, videoconferencing, etc.

- Personal: office suites.

Tricks and tips

Because of the ASP industry's novelty, companies interested in this business model should do their homework before inking any agreements. Lisa Sweet, president of Edgewood Consulting Group, a U.S. ASP advising company, identifies three steps crucial to the ASP project.

Phase I: Company management first needs to decide which applications must be managed in-house. These are usually the most critical applications related to core business skills. Next, applications most likely to produce good returns on investment if managed externally can be identified—and internal management costs compared with those offered by an ASP.

Phase II: The company then assesses its needs and seeks ASPs that can meet them. Another company's ASP experience with the same type of application may prove a valuable aid in pinpointing company requirements. However, price should not be the sole selection criterion. Will the ASP meet guaranteed service levels? What are the penalties for failure to deliver some part of a service?

Phase III: The company then defines the scope of its relationship with a selected ASP. A system should be set up to monitor ASP performance, provide early problem identification and notification, and resolve issues promptly and fairly, all the while supporting employees in their new business routines.

However, this new industry is still sorting itself out. Specific business models accommodating various customer needs may therefore not be yet available in Quebec and Canada. A review of the emerging U.S. ASP market and ongoing discussions on this subject may provide some guidance.

Concept for smaller businesses

Many IT vendors are entering this new market somewhat reluctantly as it presents a challenge to their usual business model. Nonetheless, to position themselves to cash in on the ASP market opportunity, major players have opted to collaborate with ASPs, if not adopt the model on their own.

Developers of enterprise resource planning (ERP) applications, such as SAP, PeopleSoft, Oracle, J.D. Edwards and Great Plains Software, see the ASP model as the mandatory path to business growth. After having saturated the market of large, privately owned corporations, they encountered considerable resistance trying to enter the small business market. This situation, however, is likely to improve with the introduction of outsourcing solutions. Other technology vendors are keeping their eyes on the ASP delivery model, as small business is considered likely to become the main business application arena in the early twenty-first century

First launched by USinternetworking (USi) in summer 1998, the ASP model quickly branched out and led to the creation of the ASP Industry Consortium the following spring. Dedicated to promoting the application service provider industry, this international advocacy group started with only 25 companies. However, in less than a year its ranks surpassed 400 members, with the number up to almost 500 by late 2000.

> Projections for ASP market growth vary dramatically depending on the market research company cited, since their assessments are based on different criteria. However, they all agree the market will see rapid growth in the future. IDC, the most conservative among them, predicts that in the United States, revenues of

the companies offering the most complex applications will total $2.2 billion U.S. in 2003. Gartner Group forecasts that the global ASP market could reach $22.7 billion U.S. the same year. The most optimistic of this group, Forrester Research, predicts total sales of $21 billion U.S. in 2001.

The sudden emergence of ASP is reminiscent of the information push and network computer fads that were the rage in 1996-1997. Will ASPs become the Next Big Thing—or will they follow the fate of these two trends? Some are already pointing the finger at the many pitfalls in the ASP market structure.

It is hard to forget the setbacks suffered by AT&T and Sprint in the early 1990s with similar approaches, the former offering on-line Lotus Notes services and the latter, Microsoft Back Office. Other complaints pertain to poor network reliability and the difficulties involved in ASPs meeting service level agreement commitments. Other critics argue companies will refuse to entrust third parties with control over their most strategically important applications, such as finances and R&D.

Having served a term as guinea pigs for ASP vendors looking for the right formulas, early users of these solutions express increasing satisfaction with services rendered, concludes a recent study by Zona Research. At the same time, many customers are questioning the main claim used by ASPs to lure small businesses (low service cost), insisting there are no real long-term savings. Most customers, however, agree they are glad to get technical issues off their hands.

Figure 7   Allocation of 2003 ASP market for the U.S.

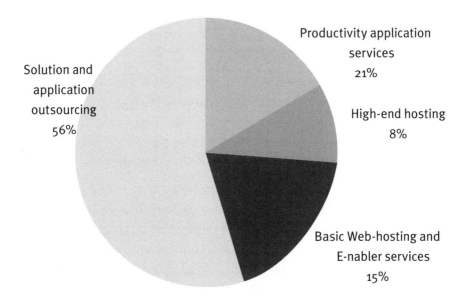

Productivity application services
21%

Solution and application outsourcing
56%

High-end hosting
8%

Basic Web-hosting and E-nabler services
15%

Deloitte Research, E-view the Internet Based ASP Marketplace, *November 1999.*

Attractive to large enterprises

ASPs insist that maturity and Internet capabilities dramatically reduce the risks associated with the approach. Nevertheless, in late 2000, most USi customers were hi-tech firms and large corporations like Hershey Foods or Herman Miller, with dedicated reliable links. They included almost no small businesses.

The ASP model is primarily attractive to large businesses and start-ups. The first group adopted this solution for less critical applications, such as email service, that would not jeopardize operations should service be interrupted for a few hours. Fast-growing start-ups are short on time and on diversified resources, and are therefore willing to play for high stakes, entrusting ASPs even with setting up their enterprise resource planning (ERP).

Virtual Networks, a manufacturer of voice and data communications systems from Sunnyvale, California, turned to Corio, a California-based ASP targeting growth companies, for access to PeopleSoft applications. Considering the costs of software purchase and internal deployment, Virtual Networks would have had to select the Great Plains Software ERP, at some 20% of the cost of PeopleSoft. However, through external outsourcing at half the price, Virtual Networks was able to afford access to the PeopleSoft package. Excite is another Corio customer for PeopleSoft, attracted by the speed of application implementation (just thirteen weeks), compared to two years for an internal deployment.

ASP solutions usually permit far less customization than in-house applications. Some companies accept this limitation because it substantially simplifies subsequent upgrades, which may prove especially painstaking in the case of tailor-made applications.

Multiple partnerships

Setting up an ASP requires multiple skills. Practically no company, whether a newcomer or a technology vendor, is able to perform all the tasks involved in remote application management. That is why many companies are building full application hosting solutions by partnering with other enterprises that complement their core skills:

- The telecommunications company Qwest joined Hewlett-Packard and SAP to offer SAP R/3 ERP services through the new ASP Qwest Cyber.Solutions (QCS). SAP works in conjunction with EDS and other firms on the same basis.

- US West teamed with Deloitte Consulting and USi to launch US West Hosting Solutions.

- Some thirty product vendors and ASPs joined Cisco Hosted Applications Initiative (CHAI), aimed at creating a new generation of routers capable of ensuring the optimization of hosted applications.

- Microsoft invested $83 million U.S. in USWeb to develop the iFrame platform—a combination of technologies for ASP solutions. Besides renting Office 2000 from its bCentral site, the Redmond giant signed deals with fifteen ASPs, turnkey manufacturers (Dell and Compaq) and telecommunications companies that can market the software application package on the same basis.

- Oracle secured the services of Qwest, British Telecommunications and Exodus Telecommunications to host its Oracle Business Online (BOL) services on their data centres. After having given BOL exclusive rights to lease its applications, Oracle reversed its decision in October 2000 and granted licences to other ASPs.

- IBM manages ERP application outsourcing by J.D. Edwards, SAP and Great Plains Software.

- FutureLink, a Calgary-based ASP that has been a sensation in California ever since it opened offices there, offers access to a full range of applications, including office software packages from Corel, for a flat monthly fee.

As we can see, approaches vary greatly among the major players. Those who become directly involved as vendors, such as Oracle and SAP, with www.mysap.com, are attracted by the alluring small-business market, which they feel is more promising than major corporations. Moreover, they wish to preserve direct relationships with end users, which would be lost if the latter no longer bought their wares.

Tricks and tips

An enterprise considering an ASP solution should first identify and specify its needs, to avoid getting lost among the wide variety of possibilities.

Model diversity

Quebec and Canadian small businesses may get a fairly good idea of the available choices by reviewing U.S.-based solutions.

- USi only implements applications for which it holds licences and does so solely on a rental basis. Unlike most ASPs, the company runs its own data centres.

- QCS can host ERPs that have already been set up by its customers, install purchased applications, or provide access to applications for a monthly fee. Sprint also offers these three options.

- Although BOL does not give access to Oracle application source codes, USi, QST, IBM and Sprint do permit a certain degree of customization. Oracle targets primarily small businesses, so it tries to cut costs to stay competitive. Its rivals, on the other hand, hope to serve large companies that demand more tailoring of systems to specific business needs.

- While the major players target companies of all shapes and sizes, many new ASPs focus on specific industries, such as manufacturing, technology, professional services, media or advertising. This trend is typified by the practices of Corio, Applicast, AristaSoft and Surebridge. Other ASPs are equally humble in their market approach and have decided to limit their services to the one or two horizontal applications they master perfectly, such as email and online billing.

Quebec

- Quebec-based ASPs launched their services in the fall of 2000 when the two largest information management system consulting firms, DMR and CGI, announced their intentions to provide ASP services.

- QuébecTel, a phone company, intends to gradually offer small businesses remote management of applications from the company's Bizznys.com portal.

- DTM Information Technology Group, a systems integrator, followed the example of numerous North American companies and also became a Canadian pioneer in the ASP market, providing MetaFrame from the U.S.-based

- Citrix company through its Nexxlink division. Citrix, a global leader in application servers accessible from workstations in large organizations, adapted its original configuration to the ASP market context. Its customers are now remotely connected via the Internet (rather than through a local network) to the appropriate server of the alliance-based network.

- Resellers, specializing in Microsoft and Oracle products' implementation are also seriously analyzing the ASP model.

Because of the unrest of the Internet market, emerging ASPs outside the United States, just like local B2B cybermarketing companies, have been enjoying a bit of a break since the spring of 2000, which has given them a chance to fine-tune their market approaches. In the fall of 2000, the instability of the developing market and the impatience of investors expecting to reap quick profits pushed the U.S. ASP market into a period of consolidation. Gartner Group predicts that by the end of the year 2001, 60% of these ASPs will be gone. Industry observers often like to recall that the automobile industry, which started with some hundred manufacturers at the beginning of the century, is now reduced to the Big Three of today.

Tricks and tips

Every aspect of the ASP initiative should be carefully considered ahead of time, since there is no easy turning back once the process is under way. While we attempted to give an overall picture of the new ASP market, the subject is too broad for one chapter.

http://www.aspnews.com/index.htm
Online ASP-related publications. The site offers news, a directory of ASP-related companies and products and articles on topics like software leasing.

http://www.erpsupersite.com
A site dedicated to ERP applications. It offers links to software
vendors, ASPs and discussion forums.

http://www.whg.org
The site of the Web Host Guild (WHG), an organization com-
prised of ASPs and software vendors. The WHG is dedicated to
raising the standards of the Web hosting industry. It has established a set of criteria for assessing service reliability, customer
support and technological skills of ASPs.

In brief

- In its purest form, the customer owns no software applications and uses the ASP application-hosting infrastructure on a pay-as-you-go basis.

- After having saturated the market of large, privately owned corporations, they encountered considerable resistance trying to enter the small business market. This situation, however, is likely to improve with the introduction of outsourcing solutions.

- Setting up an ASP requires multiple skills. Practically no company, whether a newcomer or a technology vendor, is able to perform all the tasks involved in remote application management.

Chapter 6
EDI on the Internet

In collaboration with Nicolas Duguay

As B2B e-commerce becomes more widespread, the Internet will increasingly serve as the main means for companies to do business with each other. Electronic document interchange (EDI) has existed for over twenty years and offers two advantages:

- it is based on a worldwide standard distributed in several vertical versions.

- it has earned the confidence of most large order givers.

EDI will not simply migrate to the Internet, it will evolve like all operations that move into the sphere of new technologies. A range of programming possibilities are changing EDI from a mature and relatively static technology to a dynamic environment. For instance, when combined with XML—a language used to automatically generate Web pages—EDI acquires new flexibility and sophistication while retaining the same level of reliability, due to its high level of standardization.

The Internet's broad-based, egalitarian structure has gradually transformed it from a tool controlled by big business to a decentralizing resource available to small business. The Quebec-based company Dynec is using this approach to help find a way of allowing small businesses to work together and to simplify their relations with big buyers.

Automating links between partners

As computers become increasingly commonplace, fast exchange of commercial data has become a prerequisite to the survival of companies of all sizes. Faced with a changing and uncertain environment, businesses will find it difficult to resist this general trend introduced years ago by large corporations and now available to all businesses because of the Internet.

The advent of the Computer Age has brought about a real revolution in the traditional structure of inter-company communications. New challenges and opportunities have led to the carefully planned development of a new communications system serving multiple partners within a particular supply or distribution chain.

In the 1970s, this process resulted in the birth of EDI, the Electronic Document Interchange standard. This technology, which until very recently handled eighty percent of electronic B2B exchanges, was big business's answer to problems caused by data bottlenecks.

Managing paper-based dealings in a large company can quickly turn into a major dilemma, since an estimated seventy percent of computer data transferred to paper will be eventually reprocessed within at least one other computer system. Computerizing a large share of orders between order givers and subcontractors has made it possible to partially circumvent the traditional sender/post office/recipient circuit. Not only does this method save money, is substantially boosts productivity.

Description of EDI

What is EDI?

EDI technology allows direct computer-to-computer transfers of specific kinds of data in the form of messages structured according to a predefined set of syntactic rules. EDI require a consensus on a single method of communication, so recipient computers can process data unambiguously. This condition is essential for eliminating the human factor and risks of error.

In the beginning, EDI communication standards were developed around the need of certain order givers to communicate with their partners. Each particular industry, whether food, shipping or some other sector, worked according to its own system. This was effective at the time for partners within a given industry because it responded to specific needs and functioned with a limited number of rules and commands. However, the initially drafted standards quickly faced inherent structural constraints as an increasing number of companies began operating internationally and in diverse industries.

The UN/EDIFACT standard

The need to standardize EDI transmissions around one comprehensive standard emerged from the compatibility issues that resulted from this system. The UN/EDIFACT (United Nations Electronic Data Interchange for Administration, Commerce and Transport) was adopted in 1986 to resolve international compatibility problems. While the standard has been voluntarily implemented in Europe and internationally, it has not managed to supersede North America's ANSI X12, the most widely used EDI transmission standard in most U.S.- and Canada-based industries.

UN/EDIFACT is an Esperanto of electronic document interchange. Its application to international transactions has simplified business relations that were once both complicated and costly. Prior to standardization and computerization, communications between order givers and foreign subcontractors would pass through the hands of many parties, greatly increasing the risk of error.

However, the main goal of EDI operations is not so much to reduce costs associated with repeated errors than to increase the speed of information transmission, which, in the end, leads to significant savings for all partners thanks to the reduction in inventory that can come as a result.

Just one language

The creators of the UN/EDIFACT standard considered several factors, including a specific vocabulary, an established syntax, a grammar and even rules of style. These rules allowed them to develop a real language that computers could read without human assistance. By extending the scope of the language beyond initial, small, and very specific standards, UN/EDIFACT, and ANSI X12 in North America, permit international trade between different industries.

Tower of Babel

Establishment of too strict a standard could stall implementation in new economic sectors and restrict future development. This is why the EDI architecture was conceived as an open standard and why many companies continue to feed the EDI dictionary with new industry-specific terminology.

This feature quickly developed into a real headache for EDI. In a context of increasingly interconnected companies, EDI had become a Tower of Babel. To keep a functioning EDI network as small a possible, a network's principal manager—usually a big order giver—had to make sure each and every link in the chain was equipped with complicated and expensive translation software.

Initial cost

Small businesses were therefore faced, in turn, with very high set-up costs for software and qualified personnel if they wanted to integrate EDI into their internal systems and benefit from this technology in the same ways as large organizations. But most small companies did not even bother considering such lofty arrangements. They turned down EDI from the start merely when faced with the initial costs of acquiring a reliable and secure communications link, provided by an intermediary known as a value added network (VAN). Until very recently, installation and use of this critical component was so high-priced that VANs were often blamed for poor EDI acceptance and the fact that despite their best efforts, top-of-the-line EDI order givers had been able to convert no more than eighty percent of their partners to the EDI system.

As long as VAN-connection rates remain below one hundred percent, large order givers must maintain parallel paper-based systems. This costly and redundant infrastructure is made necessary because, in an age of overspecialization, some small businesses produce irreplaceable products, putting them in a position to successfully resist pressure to adopt EDI.

The Internet changes everything

At the same time as, but independently from EDI, the Internet was established on university campuses and began to assert itself as a reliable, fast and particularly economical means of communication, soon to be discovered by the business world.

Now, most businesses of any size have Internet access and this new communications link has appeared as an economical alternative to VANs. Small businesses can now interact with large order givers much more economically than ever before.

The concept of Web-based EDI was thus born. In fact, whatever communications route data transmissions end up taking, the goal remains the same —that the information travel between senders and receivers accompanied by at least minimal security guarantees.

This is exactly the sort of thinking that led to the many EDI variants. The goal of transmitting a message from one party to another remains the same, whether over VANs, by email or even by fax. Obviously, each method of communication has its pros and cons, which will tilt the balance one way or another depending on the circumstances.

While too expensive for the smallest contenders, VANs remain the most secure and reliable transmission method, particularly in the cases of professionally well-maintained networks. The most economical method—sending EDI forms by fax—is only suited to companies that wish to operate entirely on paper-based systems without drawing any of EDI's benefits, while still meeting customer wishes. EDI by email is closer to a virtual system but the process cannot be automated because the two formats are incompatible.

If we exclude VANs or the Internet, all other EDI transmission methods are essentially improved alternatives to the good old postal system.

> In 1997, ninety-five percent of EDI traffic was handled by VANs. Many well-informed ecommerce observers feel this number will plunge to some fifty percent by 2002, with the balance handled over the Internet. When it would be so simple to switch the process to the Internet, why should VANs remain relatively un-threatened over the next couple of years? The answer is simple. The cost of setting up the networks on which VANs operate was so great that big companies are likely to continue using this still-efficient technology for some time .

However, new businesses that deploy EDI systems for doing business with their partners will probably run them over the Internet. For example, use of the Internet to transmit EDI messages skyrocketed 355% from 1997 to 1998, while the sale of Web-based EDI software also soared by nearly 300% over the same period.

While set to replace VANs as the main means of transmitting EDI data, the Internet will not operate in the same way as its predecessor. The UN/EDIFACT and ANSI X12 standards were tailored for VAN use. The rigidity and rigour inherent to EDI systems designed for fairly limited and confidential networks run counter to the primary function of the Internet. If we liken a VAN to a high-performance racetrack, the Internet must be seen as a public highway network. The Internet combines all types and qualities of roads—with the undeniable advantage of being truly global.

XML and EDI

What is XML?

The main route for developing Internet-based EDI is probably XML (extensible-language programming). XML is a first cousin of HTML, the Web's most popular document format. XML also permits the creation of executable subsets that can easily handle most existing and forthcoming dealings between businesses.

The Evolution of XML

Designed by MIT researchers at the request of the World Wide Web Consortium, XML enjoyed high credibility from its start in 1996. In early 2000, it emerged from R&D and now serves the first wave of business applications. XML's evolution parallels early developments in EDI. At its start, specialized and proprietary standards proliferated, particularly in the United States. Standardization occurred only once most of the software industry came on board. The software industry sought to speed development of the language and some players, like IBM and Microsoft, already offer XML-compliant browsing and authoring software.

In May 2000, the GCA (Graphic Communications Association) announced it was changing the name and focus of its Electronic Data Interchange Committee to the B2B Standards Committee. The new mission of this group is to develop XML versions for the forty or so EDI standards it must cover.

The advantages of XML

Generally speaking, the dynamic features of XML permit exchanges different from those of traditional EDI because they can tailor themselves to the context of each particular exchange. Classic EDI, on the other hand, lends itself more easily to pre-determined and recurrent automated transactions. This means past needs for special software and know-how are being replaced by an environment in which the application itself—be it Internet browser (current versions of Internet Explorer and Netscape 6.0 are XML-compatible), integrated management packages, and so forth—can call up the software libraries needed for EDI transactions.

The advantages of Internet-based EDI

Companies reluctant to adopt EDI because of its high set-up costs may now be tempted by the inherent benefits of the Internet-based version of this protocol.

Many large companies already provide EDI forms to their partners on their Web sites. Small businesses can simply complete these documents and transmit them over the Internet. While simple and inexpensive, this solution is nonetheless complicated for a company dealing with many different order givers on a daily basis.

> Quebec-based Dynec offers Negotium software to facilitate EDI use by retail food suppliers. Dynec's inexpensive kit and software allows an EDI link to be established between a supplier and its partners over the TCP/IP protocol. Such relations will work essentially like those of traditional EDI, except that they will provide the substantial savings of doing business over the Internet.

The only sombre note is that Internet-based EDI does not provide the same level of security as its VAN-based counterpart, in which restricted access ensures data protection. With its open structure, the Internet raises many issues pertaining to the confidentiality of data flowing through it. Rightly or wrongly, these issues raise doubts among some companies that would otherwise prefer using it to convey their EDI documents.

Data encryption and electronic signatures, however, provide for data exchanges almost as safe as those performed over VANs. While large order givers seem satisfied with this level of security for their EDI transactions, the type of solution proposed by Dynec stands every chance of attracting the attention of small businesses.

Table 3 From EDI to the e-marketplace

	EDI	Traditional B2B e-commerce	Collaborative e-commerce
Exchange	1 to 1	1 to many	Many to many
Length	Long term	Short term	Short term
Transport	Private line	Internet	Internet

Test your knowledge...

A little vocabulary

What is up-selling?

1. An Internet marketing method designed by Uppsala University.
2. The art of increasing sales and transforming clients into affiliates.
3. A method consisting of proposing additional goods and services related to an initial purchase.
   (Answer p. 126)

What is an infomediary?

1. An information broker.
2. An RCMP informer.
3. An intermediary who facilitates exchanges of information between parties to a transaction.
   (Answer p. 60)

What is an application service provider's main purpose?

1. Provide high speed Internet access.
2. Manage all or a part of companies' computer services from a distance.
3. Provide business management application software.
    (Answer p. 71)

What do you call a professional who offers his services on a site such as Guru.com or Smartworker.com?

1. An electronic nomad.
2. An e-lancer.
3. An electronic contract worker.
4. All of the above.
    (Answer chapter 7)

What does a third-party certifier do?

1. Ensure that at least one third of the total funds of a sale price are available in a buyer's bank account.
2. Deliver digital certificates and private keys, and keep the public key logs up to date.
3. Confirm before witnesses the identity of a buyer prior to an online purchase.
    (Answer p. 114)

What Canadian law on e-commerce and the protection of personal information stipulates that an electronic signature is a legal means of approving a sale?

1. B-52
2. C-6
3. C-36
    (Answer p. 150)

If you'd like to learn more...

Visit EC/EDI Info, a mega-site providing information on EDI and e-commerce, run by Integrated Technologies, a company that has developed many courses on ecommerce offered in a number of U.S. universities.
http://www.edi-info-center.com/index.html

See the FAQS on the benefits of combining the use of XML and EDI, run by the XML/EDI Group, an organization bringing together experts in e-commerce on an individual and volunteer basis for hundreds of U.S. suppliers.
http://www.xmledi-group.org/xmledigroup/answers.htm

Read "The Paper Chaser," an electronic version of an in-depth article published June 2000 in Business 2.0 magazine, on new Internet-based EDI service providers.
http://www.business2.com/content/magazine/indepth/2000/06/13/12374

In brief

- EDI will not simply migrate to the Internet, it will evolve like all operations that move into the sphere of new technologies.

- The goal of transmitting a message from one party to another stays the same, whether over VANs, by email or even by fax.

- New businesses that deploy EDI systems for doing business with their partners will probably run them over the Internet.

- Data encryption and electronic signatures provide for data exchanges almost as safe as those performed over VANs.

PART 2
TOMORROW

Chapter 7
Reshuffling E-services

In collaboration with Angélique Gridel

A team of computer programmers sold itself to the highest bidder on eBay—for $2 million U.S. The deal created a hubbub that lasted weeks and underscored one of the exciting new aspects of e-commerce—the ability to sell know-how.

Professional services do not involve complex logistics and do not require delivery. They can easily cross borders and do not have to handle returns. Situated where they are, at the crossroads of two key cyberspace trends—virtualization and globalization—they lend themselves remarkably well to Internet-based transactions.

This is not to suggest that virtual offers for services are free of problems. Such offers take on different forms depending on the specialty and the nation. Because of the large market they represent, they have, nonetheless, resulted in the establishment of numerous e-marketplaces. The central characters in such markets are known as "elancers" in America and "electronic nomads" in France. Ultimately, they are nothing more—or less—than virtual freelancers.

In this chapter, we shall provide a brief overview of how this phenomenon has already established itself among a variety of traditional and leading-edge professions. At the same time, we shall consider its likely impact on labour organization and on the "variable geometry" companies it has spawned.

Internationalization and virtualization

Internationalization and virtualization are the two pillars of the New Economy, according to many work organization specialists. As the steam engine paved the way to the industrial revolution, the Internet is transforming the economic and social landscape of the twenty-first century. Thomas Malone, professor in MIT's Sloan School of Management, has dubbed the new service sector that will emerge from this process the elance economy. kIn "The Dawn of the E-Lance Economy," published in the Harvard Business Review in the fall of 1998, Malone described this new way of organizing work.

E-lancers, or self-employed workers, are electronically linked as temporary teams to carry out specific projects. Once a project is completed, the virtual and temporary group producing it splits up. Group members head off to different missions that will link them to other individuals for the duration of a new project. The period of their joint effort can range from a day, to a month, to a year or more, after which each one once again goes his or her own way.

Virtual companies are already here

Frenchman Denis Ettighoffer, president of the Eurotechnopolis Institute, which brings together a number of large companies and institutions to study the impact of new technologies on business, refers to these networking team-mates as "electronic nomads." He characterizes them as the white collars workers of the twenty-first century, who work in conjunction with other such nomads located thousands of kilometres away. He predicts the arrival on the scene of networks of specialists and professional workers. The "diasporas" of such dispersed communities will increasingly result, he says, in the development of new products and services, rather than in permanent or structured teams.

Since Thomas Malone's article appeared in print, e-lancing has emerged from the world of the possible to become part of the increasingly virtual and online world of business. Self-employed workers, outsourcing, and telecommuting, are propagating throughout this world. Even big companies like IBM let their employees work at home or spin off into independent teams to develop specific projects.

> In Hollywood, where major studios used to reign, network-based structures have now taken the lead. Independent producers launch their own projects, put together their financial packages and surround themselves with teams of self-employed workers. These temporary "companies" disappear once a film hits the screens.

Virtual business communities

Away from the intense competition of the box office, new technologies are similarly transforming the service sectors of various industries. Professional organizations are creating virtual communities to form networks of their members and to enhance business.

Accountants

In Québec

The *Ordre des comptables agréés du Québec* decided to apply this approach in developing an Accounting Kit[11], aimed solely at other accountants and geared towards knowledge sharing. The kit includes a range of tools, including financial and accounting databases, calculators, professional directories and links to governmental and financial authorities. Its goal is three-pronged: save time by cutting paperwork, cut costs, and boost the volume and diversity of information available to members of the profession.

---

11 www.trouseca,com

With the kit, accountants who need to issue bank confirmations for small businesses can, for example, obtain the required information from secure online connections to a company's various bank accounts. New company registration forms and tax payment procedures could also be put online. If users are pleased with their initial experiences, a chartered accountants' kit for industry could ultimately be developed to meet the specific needs of corporate financial managers.

In the United States

Similar services are available to U.S. accountants, through private sites such as AccountingWeb.com[12]. In addition to providing traditional information on the profession as well as databases, it offers online training programs that users can take at their leisure, during coffee breaks or meals, for example. Site members can also register without charge for hour-long workshops on, for example, various accounting techniques, dealing with customers or taxation. During chat sessions, professionals who are willing to share their prior experiences virtually swap advice on certain kinds of tax or accounting topics.

Attorneys

In Québec

The legal profession is also heading in this direction. The *Réseau juridique du Québec*[13] is aiming to become a virtual resource centre for lawyers. It provides a list of members, professional links and a Legal Document Processor. This interactive system can be used to prepare legal documents over the Web. During the project's initial phase, only documents pertaining to personal rights—such as marriage contracts, wills and used car sales agreements—may be prepared online. The service should subsequently be extended to both small and big business.

---

12 www.accountingweb.com

13 www.avocat.qc.ca

In France

Since 1998, France's legal community has been equipped with an extranet site, *Avocaweb*[14], aimed at providing legal information to members of the profession. The site includes a messaging and navigation service, along with essential security features in view of the kind of information being shared. Intranets are to be set up for different jurisdictions, to reduce the burden involved in transmitting and managing documents, and to speed up this process along with the legal procedures themselves. With *Juricert Services*[15], the Law Society of British Columbia is also launching a pilot project to ensure secure transmission of digitally encrypted documents between lawyers and clients.

Architects

Architects, whose work often requires close cooperation among several firms, are also deploying their first virtual business communities. In line with this goal, the American Institute of Architects has created e-architect.com, providing press reviews, job offers, directories and resources for working with other members of the profession. Architects registered with ProjectGroups[16], can store their files on the site and share them with partners who can consult them, download them and complete them. A project's initial author is automatically notified of any modifications made to the original file.

Gurus, Niku and other free agents

Sites for the self-employed that seek to match personal skills with company needs are becoming pervasive. Sites like eWorkExchange[17],

---

14 www.paris.barreau.fr/Avocaweb.htm

15 www.juricert.com

16 www.punchnetworks.com/partners/earchitect

17 www.eworkexchange.com

FreeAgent.com[18], CyberWorkers.com[19], and Freelancia.com[20] are all trying to attract a wide range of experts who can attend to the needs of business, including computer programmers and consultants, Web designers and publishers, business and project management specialists, translators, creative workers, etc. Full project teams can be put together from such e-marketplaces, at least in theory.

Guru.com[21], founded in San Francisco, is one of the pioneers in this field. Its "gurus" are actually self-employed workers. But this New Age characterization is fitting, as they are also among the most dynamic and talented players on the labour market. Site members can, for example, post their profiles and promote their skills, retrieve and reply to job offers from companies, participate in chat sessions in their respective fields and virtually meet with potential team-mates. Not only does the system facilitate the process of matching supply to demand, it offers teamwork resources to its members. For example, iNiku.com[22] provides a virtual office, group agendas, file sharing, online conferencing and so forth.

A win-win formula

The benefits of e-lancing seem obvious, including an explosion in the number of interactions and jobs from around the planet and the creation of micro-enterprises offering additional skill sets. Computers and electronic networks let individuals and small businesses search for information, know-how and funding around the globe in a way that only big corporations had been able to manage until now.

Small companies are now endowed with many of the resources of big firms, while retaining small-size advantages—such as versatility, creativity and economy. With the development of communication techniques and networks, some observers are even predicting the advent of a soft-shaped, impermanent society, where e-lancers will be kings.

18 www.freeagent.com
19 cyberworkers.com
20 freelancia.com
21 www.guru.com
22 www.iniku.com

Cost reduction

Companies, and small businesses in particular, will benefit from e-lancing by cutting the cost of services and by acquiring access to a mobile and broader pool of skills than in the past. The industrial era was nurtured by the simplification of communications and transactions brought by the appearance of the railroad, the telegraph system, telephones and faxes. Nowadays, information and communications technologies (ICT) make it easier to take care of a variety of tasks outside a company, at lesser cost.

Information transmittal

Information may be instantaneously and economically transmitted to a large number of users. Vertical portals are gradually achieving higher success rates than employment agencies, where commissions may equal as much as 30% of wages paid to contract workers. Elancers can use such sites to find new jobs or projects and to extend their networks outside their usual geographic regions. According to the creators of Elance.com[23], 40% of these types of transactions are already taking place outside the United States—and their pace will pick up with globalization.

> In 1998, Thomas Malone wrote about Topsy Tail, a beauty accessories manufacturer that achieved all its production through outside resources. The company was able to earn $80 million U.S. in sales with only three employees . . . and without ever having to handle any product. All phases of the business were delegated to subcontractors, including injection moulding firms for manufacturing, designers to create product packaging, as well as distributors and independent sales dealers. This way, the company was able to focus its efforts on new product development and marketing strategies.

23 www.e-lance.com

Flexibility

By releasing highly skilled team members and letting them temporarily carry out other projects at remote locations, companies also obtain another competitive advantage. Work can be done in a more flexible and efficient manner than in traditional settings. Projects can be reorganized to follow the evolution of the market or of new technologies.

Recruiting

Companies no longer have to worry about finding the right people for the right slots and can instead focus on their core activities. E-lancing will also redefine career opportunities, which we can expect in the future to be oriented more around general directions than specific functions. Job seekers will no longer aim at holding one job within a single company, but at acquiring a set of experiences and skills that can be applied to one project after another. For those who continue to work within just one company, possibilities for promotion will still exist, but on a much more limited basis.

Many ways to earn our keep

Cutting costs does not mean eliminating them. E-lancing clearly comes at a price for its practitioners.

User costs

Most start-up e-marketplaces offer member services for free. Once their formulas have been tried and tested, however, they can begin charging monthly fees or package rates for services provided, such as online training, virtual meetings and file sharing. When a contract is signed between an e-lancer and a company, the latter usually pays the site a 5% to 10% commission. Some sites split fees between e-lancers and companies or require flat fees upon project submission.

A different sort of competition

Service-oriented e-marketplaces are leading to a new type of relations on the labour market—a globalized market in which skills and services have their price. Some hundred skilled self-employed workers may compete to win one job. An online auction system that can help define the value of a project or a specialist is evolving. E-lance.com has set up a "dynamic" price-setting system that works like a reverse auction. Self-employed workers bid competitively to win jobs. This service could eventually push service prices down.

Some e-lancers complain of the threat presented by online marketplaces from European- or Southeast Asian-based professionals in their fields offering ridiculously low rates. The proliferation of such e-marketplaces could result in a fight to the finish, with the less talented left behind in the dust. The American site Ants.com[24] offered a $100,000 U.S. reward at its launch to anyone referring qualified e-lancers. The more enterprising can also launch their own commission-generating sites by recruiting experts in the most sought-after fields.

In the United States, where ethical rules are often murkier than those of Canada or Europe, sites like SharkTank[25] and LegalMatch[26] get lawyers to compete and offer their best rates to clients. The competition is open and raises ethical questions. Any number of lawyers, for example, can view the rates offered by colleagues for a trademark registration request and adjust their own rates accordingly, knowing they are not bound by their offers. By the same token, clients can reject even the lowest bidders. The sites' owners are compensated with commissions paid by the lawyers. This system, however, flies in the face of the legal principle espoused by some experts that attorneys are solely accountable to their clients.

24 www.ants.com

25 www.sharktank.com

26 legalmatch.com

Is there an executive in the house?

Transition to e-lancing has an as-yet unmeasured social cost to it. This new way of doing business essentially involves rethinking the management process. The challenge for companies hiring such e-lancers is to properly manage these new partners—in addition to managing the talents of their own staff.

How can virtually organized projects bear fruit without the benefits of a mastermind or central management? The Internet is the product of joint contributions, organized by no single individual. This means company executives can no longer play the same roles—if indeed there is any role left for them to play. Individuals will organize themselves and coordinate their own work. Decentralization does not mean no one will be in charge, but that responsibilities will pass from one person to another within the course of a given project. In other words, rules of the game must be established, with standards set up that can govern all aspects of different transactions, including contracts, proprietary systems, dispute settlement and so forth.

Some e-marketplaces are already offering solutions and procedures designed to establish a "corporate culture" extending well beyond the framework of an individual project to a set of short- or medium-term joint undertakings. However, all those working together must share the same sense of responsibility, the same work ethic and a similar operating procedure. Such a model would be neither very effective nor affordable if all work organization details had to be renegotiated for each new project and for each new person who joins a team.

> Scoring systems are being developed to avoid disputes and to monitor the quality of service rendered. E-Lance.com lets e-lancers and contractors assess each party's performance at the end of a job. The company arbitrates in the event of a dispute, particularly with respect to payment. To avoid such conflicts, Smarterwork.com[27] has set up an online payment system. After selecting an expert, the contractor deposits the agreed amount

---

27 www.smarterwork.com

in an escrow account until the goods are delivered. This way, the company serves as a reliable intermediary—or "trusted third-party," in the new e-commerce jargon.

This model suggests that the professional services of the twenty-first century will be totally unlike those of the previous one. Professional mobility and skill sharing will make it possible to resolve the complexity of needs and of exchanges.

Everything is now in place—or on the way to becoming so—for the advent of an elance economy. This includes broadband networks, data-swapping standards, groupware, e-payments and micro-venture capital markets. But what will we do with this economy? The more prosperity and fre6edom this new system provides professional workers and those using their services, the more it may also alienate them—by increasing competition to the point that it seriously diminishes the quality of life for e-lancers. If that is true, e-marketplaces of self-employed workers will turn out to be no better than slave markets.

If you'd like to learn more...

Visit the site of the Harvard Business Review, and read The Dawn of the ELance Economy.
http:www.hbsp.harvard.edu/products/hbr/sepoct98/98508.htmlo

In brief

- One of the exciting new aspects of e-commerce is the ability to sell know-how.

- Professional organizations are creating virtual communities to form networks of their members and to enhance business.

- Sites for the self-employed that seek to match personal skills with company needs are becoming pervasive.

- With the development of communication techniques and networks, some observers are even predicting the advent of a soft-shaped, impermanent society, where e-lancers will be kings.

- Service-oriented e-marketplaces are leading to a new type of relations on the labour market—a globalized market in which skills and services have their price.

CHAPTER 8
E-COMMERCE'S KEY
INTERMEDIARIES AND PARTNERS

In collaboration with Angélique Gridel

Business-to-business e-commerce transactions are often more complex than those typical of retail trade. They usually bring into play not just sellers and buyers, but a range of intermediaries and partners.

Payments may involve one or more financial institutions, especially when amounts are large.

International transactions often require the services of one or more certification bodies to securely identify buyers and to guarantee their credibility or solvency.

All goods must be shipped in compliance with customs regulations and laws of those countries involved. Support in this process must be provided by partners specializing in these fields.

Governments will also be involved, even in the virtual universe of e-commerce. Regulations must be applied and taxes collected. Governments may even participate actively as buyers or sellers of products and services.

In this chapter, we will examine the various third parties involved in ecommerce transactions, such as banks, certification agencies, government bodies, and support service providers.

Online banks to the rescue of small business

Banks have begun to appreciate the value of B2B e-commerce, particularly as demand on their traditional services has stagnated.

Banks are well positioned to play a leading role as B2B e-commerce service providers because of the long and intimate relationships they have developed with business over the years. Apart from transposing their traditional services to the online world, banking institutions will be fulfilling new roles specific to e-commerce, beginning with certification[28] and extending to the management of e-marketplaces[29].

> The financial applications market is virtually wide open. According to an eBanking study by eMarketer, only 4.2 million of 18 billion invoices were processed online by late 1999. Small business represents a considerable potential market for banks in this and similar fields. And small businesses, which usually cannot afford full-time computer specialists, require more than just financial services.

Online competition

With new financial intermediaries springing up on the Internet, competition is so fierce that banks will be forced to offer online services that extend beyond their usual product line. The U.S.' Office of the Comptroller of Currency has granted bank status to various online establishments, allowing them to do business without being linked to brick-and-mortar institutions. Japan Bank Net is the first online financial institution in Japan to be given approval to operate as a bank.

---

28 See section below on certification services.

29 See Chapter 4.

After an initial period of watchfulness, where, for once, American banks were as cautious as their colleagues internationally, the great banks of the world launched themselves headlong into the pursuit of e-commerce business.

> Germany's Deutschebank, for example, plans to invest over one billion euros per year in its Internet activities. The Deutschebank intends to offer clearing, settlement, currency exchange, certification, financing, commission-collection and risk-management services.

If they wish to enjoy a full share of the windfall being generated by e-commerce, banks should position themselves in specific niches and offer a wider array of services to small business within broad-based or vertical e-marketplaces. Such services would include providing advice on doing business over the Internet, procurement of office supplies at preferred rates, supply of legal documents (by teaming with attorneys) and so forth. Canadian banks and financial institutions have begun furnishing services oriented to the needs of small business. The struggle for customer loyalty is likely to be intense, as such enterprises will not hesitate to go elsewhere if the offer is more attractive.

Canadian examples

> The Canadian International Bank of Commerce (CIBC) intends to assert itself as a business and resource network for small business. The bank estimates small businesses can save up to two thousand dollars per year through two specific offers. Traditional banking services such as deposits, withdrawals, transfers, cheques and invoice payments will be provided without charge through its bizsmart.com[30] portal. And the portal's ecommerce division will feature partnerships with companies such as Staples (Bureau en Gros in Quebec) and Chapters, offering discounts to small business.

---

30 www.bizsmart.com

In a similar vein, the Bank of Montreal has allied itself with NewSys Solutions, an Ottawa-based news and communications company, to launch regional online business centres. These centres will provide small business with local news, technical literature, management tools and software, and e-commerce transaction services.

Scotiabank's scotiawebstore.com[31] provides online means for small businesses to create their own e-commerce sites. The bank walks users through the process, from entering a company name and selecting a design and concept for a product catalogue to providing billing in Canadian or U.S. currency. Setting up a site costs $150 and monthly fees vary from $100 to $150, depending on site size. Purchasers are assured that all credit card information is handled by the bank and not by the business in question. The Toronto Dominion Bank, on the other hand, provides a list of Web site designers for small businesses that wish to set up their own sites.

Canada's smallest bank, the Laurentian, decided it should find a special niche to fight the competition. The Laurentian became the first financial institution in North America to provide financial products wholesale over the Internet through its subsidiary, B2B Trust.

Banks will still have to deal with competition from new contenders that use the Internet to resolve typical B2B problems arising from dealing with more than one bank. Payment solutions for products or services provided through e-commerce will remain limited until the fall of 2000, even though Internet-based technologies will eventually handle the more complex online transactions. Credit cards in particular are not suited for business-to-business transactions and certain companies have specialized in providing integrated payment services for B2B transactions.

---

31 www.scotiawebstore.com

American example

> The American Ariba portal[32] has teamed with financial institu-
> tions to provide a central meeting place for buyers, suppliers
> and financial institutions. All partners will be able to integrate
> a wide range of financial products issued by the financial institu-
> tions of their choice into their business practices.

Third-party certification services

A world of paperless transactions between parties who have no physical contact and usually do not even know each other is radically different from that of traditional commercial exchanges. This is particularly true in e-commerce, where the amounts involved are usually higher and the products and services exchanged can be of strategic value to participants.

According to Deloitte & Touche of Toronto, online deals average $75,000, which means certain guarantees must be provided. Buyer identity must be assured, plus the seller needs to be certain the buyer will not refuse a transaction once committed to it. Paper-based guarantees are possible, but recourse to them would defeat the speed and automation of the Internet.

E-signatures alone or with digital certification are gaining ground. Even lawyers— usually adamant about having "something on paper"—have rallied to their cause. The insurance, pharmaceutical, medical and manufacturing industries are all adopting this trend. Digital signatures will soon be as common as email.

Firms such as RSA, Entrust and Canada's Certicom provide the basic technical tools for generating digital signatures and certificates, accompanied by the security envelopes needed to make messages tamper-proof[33]. However, these assurances are not enough. Who will guarantee

---

32 www.ariba.com

33 See Chapter 12 on transaction security.

a party's identity or the fact a party is qualified to perform the transaction in question?

This is where third-party certifiers come into play. The main function of these organizations is to deliver the digital certificates and private keys needed for online commerce. The most reliable provide certificates issued solely in the presence of their holders, this high level of authentification sometimes required in the case of very large transactions.

Third-party certifiers are responsible for maintaining a directory of public customer keys and keeping this directory accessible to outside parties. Naturally, any certificates issued must comply with a national and an international key infrastructure to permit cross-certification between parties located in different countries.

Public or private

In North America, digital certificates are usually handled by (private) technical parties pursuant to fairly formal agreements and a relatively loose government-imposed framework.

> In the United States, Digital Signature Trust issues letters
> of credit that guarantee the identity of online individuals.
> Montreal-based SILANIS Technology has developed ApproveIt,
> a digital signature, and KYBERPASS, of Ottawa, has created
> Identrus digital-signature, aimed at businesspersons. Verisign
> and its Quebec-based sponsor, VPN Tech, are also prominent in
> this field.

Internationally, the situation is quite different. Legal and legislative frameworks vary from nation to nation. Differences are even apparent between Canada and the U.S. Ottawa tends to take direct action[34]. Washington, on the other hand, tends to leave such issues in the hands of business.

Differences elsewhere can be more pronounced. In many countries, particularly those of Europe, the private sector is not trusted in these

---

34 As with Bill C-6 on the protection of private information and the federal government's establishment of a national public key infrastructure.

matters. In France, for instance, only groups enjoying "official" status, such as banks, notaries and institutions (i.e., France's national research institute, the CNRS) are permitted to act as certifiers.

Tricks and tips

Any company wishing to enter the field of e-commerce, particularly on an international basis, must find one or more partners that understand the field and are equipped to handle the technical, regulatory and financial problems of certification. This may require more than one partner, as there is no guarantee one provider alone can take care of all details.

Government is open for e-business

Enacting national legislation before uniform international rules are in place has two effects. Consumers and business are placing greater trust in e-signatures and governments are speeding their transition into the digital age. After B2B, B2G (business to government) is the next promising market for investment.

E-government increases the efficiency of the administrative process and reduces transaction costs. Designed primarily so citizens can pay income and sales taxes, the same services are also available to businesses, which not only pay taxes but may also provide goods and services to government. Potential savings for government are huge. Some large companies report spending 20% less per year with Internet-based procurement. Experts predict the U.S. government could save $110 billion U.S. per year.

Developing the right exchanges

The U.S. is home to Internet-based B2G pioneers. France paved the way a decade ago with its Minitel service but failed to export the concept. Citizens in Indiana have been able since 1996 to pay fines online, file permit requests and search for legal documents such as criminal cases or vital records. Pricewaterhouse Coopers reports that 32% of Canadian Netizens used the Internet to access government, and particularly provincial, services in 1999.

The Quebec tax department (*ministère du Revenu du Québec*) is a good example of this phenomenon. Its EDI and data acquisition promotion group is busy developing online payment systems. This is a win-win situation for both business and government. Benefits include increased productivity, savings in time and money, reduced delays in data processing and better efficiency.

Revenue Québec has allied itself with many partners to develop the technological aspects of tools and processes primarily aimed at electronic transfers with large Canadian financial institutions. In January 1993, for instance, the National Bank of Canada payroll department became the first to electronically process wage deductions.

Ever the ally of small business, the Caisses Populaires Desjardins came on board in the summer of 2000 with 2,500 transactions in August and 5,000 in September. Payroll deductions, sales taxes, tax instalments, taxes due and alimony payments can all presently be made online.

In the 1999 to 2000 period, Revenue Québec recorded over 600,000 electronic payment transfers valued at $6.4 billion. Compare this to 1992-1993, with 7,200 similar transactions worth just $7 million.

The person responsible for developing these services at Revenue Québec is the first to admit much time and many phases will be involved before the state becomes actively involved in B2B transactions. A broad-based governmental electronic transfer system must overcome many hurdles and delays because of stodgy government machinery, mired in regulatory traps and administrative requirements.

Early birds do get the worms

According to Don Tapscott, Canadian promoter of the new economy and president of the Digital 4 Sights task force, governments have every interest to quickly change their attitudes. If government agencies do not fundamentally restructure themselves to meet the challenges of the new economy, civil society and the business world will look for and find alternatives to government's traditional services to take advantage of the speed and ease resulting from the digital age.

Financial institutions are also under the same gun. At the present time, small business is learning to deal with B2G. Banks, benefiting from customer trust, can provide useful assistance by offering e-payment services. Unfortunately, some banks have proved quite hesitant to jump into the fray.

Banks want to improve customer service because of their unflagging attachment to maintaining the kind of large volumes needed to keep costs down. Banks occasionally balk at the thought of developing programs and software themselves, or in conjunction with government agencies, to facilitate electronic transfers between their customers and federal or provincial tax departments.

Banks could end up paying dearly for such economies of scale. Many companies, and especially start-ups, are keenly interested in the technical protocols issued by government agencies. These companies have the financial resources and technical means to insert e-payment procedures in their accounting software. Financial institutions could end up as waypoints, rather than major crossroads, in the B2G chain.

Small business has been even slower to adopt online payment, with fear over the "Y2K Bug" paralysing many such initiatives. The spectre has faded but habits die hard. The mindset has yet to accept the concept of e-government.

Executives and managers from a previous generation are even more reluctant to trust their destinies to virtual reality. Without tangible proof of payment and unsure of transaction security, they resist electronic transmission of forms and payments.

Hesitation over e-signatures and other methods of certification is even greater. Just one success story from a small businessperson will convince far more other businesses to deal online with the government than all the pamphlets and brochures a government agency can produce.

Calling all suppliers

After many successful pilot projects, the Clinton administration launched a major plan to encourage the emergence of e-government. This plan was aimed at citizens and small businesses in need (unlike large companies) of training wheels to get rolling on the Information Highway.

The portal Firstgov.gov[35] will feature a simple online form to let businesses of any size respond to calls to tender. This alluring target market represents $300 billion U.S. in subsidies and $200 billion U.S. in procurements. Designed to save its customers money, Firstgov.gov will also give small businesses a chance to prove their mettle. By the year 2003, all government purchases will be made online.

This has naturally attracted some big players like IBM, Lockheed Martin, and KPMG. Systems integrators are offering to host the administrative services of the various state, county and municipal levels of government. The largest supplier of government services solutions for the Internet, NIC (National Information Consortium), has teamed with Deloitte Consulting to offer online procurements systems throughout the world.

The market is sufficiently large to allow start-ups like ezgov.com[36] or GovWorks[37] to place their solutions online. These start-ups are opening portals and offering specialized software free of charge. They generate revenue through transaction fees charged either to the government or to the user.

This solution is particularly suitable to local governments with limited budgets and a desire to avoid frequent system updates. Exgov, for instance, charges from one to five dollars per transaction, which the

35 www.firstgov.gov

36 www.ezgov.com

37 www.govworks.com

government can elect to pay or pass on to the user. Other companies, such as Igov.com, are banking on the $18 billion U.S. spent each year by the U.S. federal government on procurements not requiring tenders, for items like computer products and stationery supplies.

New logistics for the New Economy

With business taking place in the New Economy at the speed of light, deliveries must be sped up to follow suit. Online logistics will play a big strategic role that will prove much more crucial than that of banks, third-party certifiers or governments. Net profits will be that much higher if delivery services are fine-tuned.

What now matters is not so much the product as the delivered product. Shipping the product is only half the work. Information must now be transmitted so customers can track their parcels in real time. Such tracking services are now available over cell phones and electronic organizers.

> According to Forrester Research, deliveries of online purchases including e-tailing and B2B transactions will rise 20% annually, from three billion dollars in 1999 to $6.5 billion in 2003. This amount could be even higher since Forrester tends to be conservative in its estimates. No other segment of the transport industry is likely to experience such explosive growth.

E-logistics must be prepared to respond to three basic issues. Where is my order? Can I change my order? When will my order be shipped? Because of the volume of data to be transmitted and the complexity of e-commerce networks, more money can be made by outsourcing logistics operation to 3PLs, or Third Party Logistics providers.

> Descartes Systems Group[38] is a pioneer in the field of Internet-based global logistics networks. This Ontario company launched its Internet strategy in October 1998 to provide maximum shipping efficiency to consignors of goods, recipients of goods and shipping firms. Descartes Systems Groups earns its

---

38 www.descartes.com

income from fees charged to new customers joining the network.

The industry leader is clearly i2, an American provider of
online logistics software for large companies. Together with
TradeMatrix[39], i2 offers to handle online logistics for e-marketplaces. TradeMatrix's integrated systems, which electronically
manage exchanges between shippers, transportation companies, forwarders, customs brokers, etc., are particularly used in
air shipping, metallurgy and retail trade.

Added value is the key to success. The companies most likely to succed
will be the ones that offer the greatest number of complementary
services, such as computing the total cost of logistical support, automatic notification of delays, real-time calculation of duty payments and
so forth. Many companies lump all these services and provide them
through full-service portals, such as the ones listed above.

Net-Transport offers customized logistics solutions on its
Logistics-Net.com[40] site. Manugistics has developed an online
commercial network for Canadian Tire and all of its key suppliers. Etruck.net[41] and National Transportation Exchange (NTE[42])
use their sites to put consignors of goods in touch with shipping
firms to facilitate emergency shipments, knowing that 30% of
the U.S. trucking fleet is rolling empty.

Celarix has developed its iSuite to ensure the compatibility of
systems and follow-up procedures. iSuite is an Internet database used to collect data from sellers, manufacturers, shipping
companies and supplier warehouses. Once adopted by most
users, these systems will perform so efficiently they might very
well replace the less flexible EDI system used by shipping companies up until now.

39 www.tradematrix.com

40 www.logistics-net.com

41 www.etruck.net

42 www.nte.net

Logistics is also one of the sectors where the application service provider (ASP) formula[43] will attract the attention of small business. Most lack expertise in logistics and may find the idea of an expert supplying this service appealing.

E-logistics offers increased operational control, allowing businesses to offer improved services at reduced prices. It is readily apparent that, among the thousand or so B2B e-marketplaces that have appeared on the Internet in 1999 and 2000, the ones that have included logistics among their services will have the best chances of success. In the arena of ecommerce, logistics has become the weapon with which to clobber the competition.e

In brief

- Business-to-business e-commerce transactions are often more complex than those typical of retail trade. They usually bring into play not just sellers and buyers, but a range of intermediaries and partners.

- If they wish to enjoy a full share of the windfall being gene-rated by e-commerce, banks should position themselves in specific niches and offer a wider array of services to small business within broad-based or vertical e-marketplaces.

- Third-party certifiers are responsible for maintaining a direc-tory of public customer keys and keeping this directory acces-sible to outside parties.

- E-logistics offers increased operational control, allowing busi-nesses to offer improved services at reduced prices.

- In the arena of ecommerce, logistics has become the weapon with which to clobber the competition.

43 See Chapter V on outsourcing.

CHAPTER 9
INTERACTIVE MARKETING: USING THE NET TO GROW

Yves Leclerc, Angélique Gridel, Mathieu Locas, Mario Pelletier

Internet-based B2B marketing offers an unprecedented host of possibilities. Communication is cheap and easy, with target audiences located across the street or thousands of miles away. Better yet, the Internet's interactivity makes it easier to sharply focus marketing efforts and it provides an excellent springboard for the sort of one-to-one marketing envisioned by Don Peppers and Martha Rogers in their 1993 book, The One-to-One Future.

The Internet's aptitude for direct B2B marketing is a function of the strong worldwide growth in the number of online businesses. For the first time, in 1999, more than half of all small American and Canadian businesses have Internet access. Similar online growth is being echoed with a slight delay by developed European and Asian nations.

Interactive marketing has become an integral element of all promotional strategies. Online B2B advertising purchases grew by 450% from 1999 to 2000, according to Jupiter Communications and Media Metrix. The click-through banner is the most popular form of such publicity, representing 50% of all online advertising. However, we expect this share to shrink as new interactive marketing models that are better targeted at small businesses and better suited to their budgets percolate through to the surface.

We will examine the advantages of using the Internet for marketing, including its global reach, its ability to find new prospects and develop customer loyalty, and its capacity for using specific channels in sales and in marketing. We will survey the approaches and tools available and analyze how a set of separate strategies can be deployed to achieve maximum benefits.

The theory of the 4 Ps

Any e-marketplace that wants to succeed must provide custom service. E-marketplaces that astutely apply the wealth of direct marketing tools made possible by the interactivity and global reach of the Internet will be well-positioned to survive when competition forces a thinning of their ranks.

Tricks and tips

Whatever the strategy, the traditional keys to good marketing, i.e., the 4 Ps—Product, Price, Position and Promotion—should always take front row seats. Businesses should always know what they are selling, at what cost, in what way and through which distribution channel. They should also know which market is targeted for their sales, to avoid diluting their efforts through costly and ineffective operations.

Finding and retaining customers

The Internet is not only the perfect tool for finding and retaining customers and partners, it is an inexhaustible source of information. It provides many sophisticated applications for optimizing the process of finding new customers. It would be a big mistake to rely solely on a company Web site for finding new prospects.

Email advertising

Regular postal advertising generates response rates of 2% to 4%. Well-targeted advertising by email, on the other hand, generates response rates of 5% to 10%. Email ads that have been requested by customers are even more effective. In the case of e-tail commerce, ITM Strategies reports that email requested by consumers is five times more profitable than direct email, and twenty times more effective than banner advertising. Response rates for B2B mailings should be the same as or higher than those for consumer mailings.

Spam—or mass unsolicited email advertising—on the other hand, can do more harm than good. As intolerance to this practice has grown with the rise in email advertising, more and more consumers and business are closing their doors to such solicitations. This is why companies must urgently enter into personal relationships with their customers to get prior permission to contact them by email. An email operation will only be effective when well targeted and based on appropriate mailing lists.

Email address lists

Email address lists are sold in the U.S. for around $250 to $300. The best include the email addresses of those who are willing to receive emailed advertisements. Many networks are dedicated to this type of opt-in email. YesMail[44], a leader in the field, has the email addresses of eight million people willing to receive offers or who have expressed interest

---

44 www.yesmail.com

in particular topics. A dedicated search engine, lists.com[45], catalogues hundreds of thousands of such mailing lists.

Tricks and tips

> Building a potential customer list is a worthwhile effort for business-to-business marketing. One of the best ways of doing this is to offer free emailed newsletters. Subscribers interested in receiving information on specific topics or services are excellent candidates for direct marketing. Responses rates from advertisements inserted in special interest newsletters are generally higher than those from banner advertising, despite the latter's popularity.

Content

For a Web site to be an effective marketing tool, it must do more than simply provide general information. Value-added services will convert visitors into buyers and regular customers. To build lasting relationships, exchanges must be personalized, in line with two basic approaches. The first is to maintain a constant relationship with large accounts, to keep a watch on their evolving needs, to provide information on products and services and so forth. The second is to convert occasional customers into regular ones by encouraging them to make a larger share of purchases with the company doing the soliciting. Upselling—or proposing goods and services related to an initial purchase—is one good way of promoting repeat business.

---

45 www.lists.com

Make it personal

With its unprecedented capacity for narrowly targeting a customer base, the Web makes it possible to enter into one-to-one relationships with individuals and companies and to respond to their most pressing needs. Close one-to-one relationships allow all parties to cultivate business relationships and build long-lasting bonds. Email, for instance, enables easy private and personal exchanges. With the right database, a company can respond to specific needs and provide individual answers to requests for information by formulating custom content at a moment's notice.

One sector of software development focusing on customer relations management (CRM) aims at partially or completely automating the customer follow-up process. Some of these tools, like those of industry leader Broadvision, are very sophisticated and usually quite costly. However, new CRM software better suited to the price and performance requirements of small business is beginning to appear.

> Amazon.com was one of the first companies to take full advantage of the Internet's customization abilities. A customer's reading preferences are carefully noted during an initial purchase, making it easy to follow-up with book and promotional offerings tailored to the customer's profile.

E-tailing is not the only sector where one-to-one marketing is possible. It is just as important—and possible—to follow the same approach in B2B marketing. Purchasing responds primarily to company needs. All things being equal, the choice of one supplier over another depends on the personal feelings and business perceptions of the person placing the order and any influence exerted on this individual by coworkers.

Tricks and tips

Customizing relationships increases the odds of building lasting bonds based on confidence and mutual understanding. The Internet makes it possible to maintain relationships with major customers and to inform them of new products or promotional offers by email or over a Web site.

Companies that make online B2B sales are not successful in these efforts solely because they give good prices. The range of products offered and the benefits they provide customers are equally important.

Playing the information card with style

"Content" usually means information on a product or company. However, company Web sites can also provide humour, weather reports, discussion groups—and more. To make a Web site more exciting, a supplier of rebuilt laser toner cartridges can host chat forums on eco-friendly office practices or on energy savings at work.

Small businesses that monitor the frequency of customer purchases can also provide customized information to their buyers with the aim of turning them from occasional customers into regular ones. If an office supply company, for example, knows that a customer firm buys its paper supplies every three months, it can send a customized email offering a discount a few weeks before purchasing decisions are made.

Information on products and services is important because customers are thirsty for knowledge. E-tail and B2B customers are seeking, evaluating and comparing information. More and more tools are available to meet such needs and some even perform these tasks automatically. For example, a small translation firm could provide price and service comparison charts, while underscoring the fact that its higher prices are offset by the better quality it provides. Informed and interested customers are in the driver's seat. Competitors are never more than a mouse click away on the Internet. Fulfilling—and even more importantly, foreseeing—the need for information is even more important over the Internet than it is in traditional business.

> Live, online events such as clinics, conferences, seminars, and workshops, provide opportunities to broadcast information on products and services and to seek new customers. Expensive and technologically complex online events should not be a goal in and of themselves. Online conferences will only yield benefits if their content is top-notch and if any contacts they produce are pursued. For example, Intraware[46] invites selected participants to online conferences and gives them one free hour of consulting services tailored to their needs.

Immediate answers to online questions

Customers have greater confidence in companies that respond quickly to their requests for information. Experts agree that the maximum delay for replying to queries is forty-eight hours except, of course, in the case of major customers, where responses should be immediate. Interest in a product or service wanes with time. Buyers tend to favour sellers who provide desired information promptly.

In its simplest form, digital information is provided by email accompanied by pertinent Web links or attached documents. However, companies must first make sure their customers are willing to receive email before they send it.

New technologies permitting automated response systems mean this process can now work more smoothly. Automatic replies can be generated for Web site queries using well-programmed software that reduces the need for human responses to special cases.

---

46 www.intraware.com

Tricks and tips

Web sites can make it faster and easier to update information, such as catalogues tailored to a specific customer profile. Optimal customized relationships, though, must be integrated into a company's sales, billing, logistics and other systems.

Getting hitched

Partnerships and alliances make it possible to considerably cut marketing and sales costs for Internet-based relationships, just as they do in traditional business practices. In the field of computers, for instance, suppliers use alliances to encourage purchase of a full range of products, rather than just a single item. Adapting existing partnership models to the Internet does not go far enough. The medium offers new possibilities that should be explored.

Affiliate programs, in which traffic is sent to another site as part of a revenue-sharing scheme, are the most widespread alliance formulas used in interactive marketing. The affiliate becomes a sort of agent or distributor, receiving a commission whenever a customer, referred to the program site by the affiliate site, purchases a product.

A company should prudently choose from among the hundreds of available affiliate programs. This means checking a program's legitimacy, testing and evaluating it, and making sure visitors are satisfied with services provided. Companies well-versed in e-commerce could also create their own such programs.

A program promoter's main objective, naturally, is to boost revenues without increasing costs. Achieving this goal means responding to the needs of major customers, affiliate partners and secondary customers (the partner's customers). The program should be seen as a business rather than simply as a marketing tool. This means paying constant attention to and showing consistent interest in the program. A legal agreement is essential, as many partners may be involved. All such partners should be aware of the terms of the agreement before entering into any such affiliations.

It is impossible to cover all the possibilities offered by interactive online B2B marketing in just one chapter. The Internet is an inexpensive laboratory for experimentation in which marketing methods are only limited by the imagination. The proof lies in the many sites that have become involved in this field.

If you'd like to learn more...

Read the B2B section of the Advertising Age site.
http://www.netb2b.com/

Subscribe to a weekly newsletter on B2B marketing.
http://e-newsletters.internet.com/b2bmarketing.html

Visit the B2B marketing section on the site of Marketing Sherpa, a marketing e-zine.
http://www.b2bmarketingbiz.com/

Visit the B2B e-commerce section of the ClickZ site.
http://clickz.com/cgi-bin/gt/cz/index.html?track=111

Visit the B2B marketing resources centre on the site of the American Business Marketing Association.
http://www.marketing.org/learning/library.html

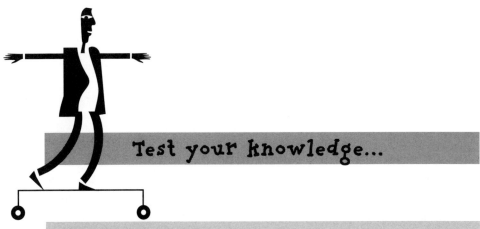

Test your knowledge...

Striking dates and examples

Since when, in Quebec, are facsimiled documents considered acceptable proof in a court of law?

1. 1990
2. 1996
3. 1994
   (Answer p. 150)

In 1999, how much did Canadian companies spend on passive security systems?

1. $500 million
2. $1 billion
3. $12 billion
   (Answer p. 165)

As of summer 2000, what percentage of companies between 20 to 49 employees had Internet access?

1. 50%
2. 65%
3. 77%
   (Answer p. 176)

As of summer 2000, what percentage of American small businesses had Internet access?

1. 50%

2. 65%

3. 85%

(Answer p. 176)

According to a poll by the Canadian Federation of Independent Business, what percentage of companies had a Web site as of summer 2000?

1. 10%

2. 15%

3. 21%

(Answer p. 176)

B2B represents what percentage of commercial exchanges in the U.S.?

1. 1% to 5%

2. 5% to 10%

3. 10% to 15%

(Answer p. 176)

In brief

- Any e-marketplace that wants to succeed must provide custom service.

- This is why companies must urgently enter into personal relationships with their customers to get prior permission to contact them by email. An email operation will only be effective when well targeted and based on appropriate mailing lists.

- One of the best ways of building a potential customer list is to offer free emailed newsletters.

- To build lasting relationships, exchanges must be personalized, in line with two basic approaches: maintain a constant relationship with large accounts and convert occasional customers into regular ones.

- Fulfilling—and even more importantly, foreseeing—the need for information is even more important over the Internet than it is in traditional business.

- Customers have greater confidence in companies that respond quickly to their requests for information.

- Partnerships and alliances make it possible to considerably cut marketing and sales costs for Internet-based relationships, just as they do in traditional business practices.

CHAPTER 10
IMPORT AND EXPORT ON THE INTERNET: TAKING THE STEP IN GOOD COMPANY

In collaboration with Angélique Gridel and Yan Barcelo

All encompassing and planet-wide, the Internet eliminates the obstacle of distance and offers virtually unlimited possibilities to the business sector. Now in its formative phase at the turn of the millennium, e-commerce must fulfill at least some of its promise before it can provide small business with instant and spontaneous access to international markets.

Presently, the very large majority of business-to-business (B2B) transactions occur within national and regional boundaries. Barriers to the development of online import-export are many. These barriers are cultural and extend beyond the language barrier, having more to do with local business habits and customs. The barriers are also regulatory in nature, because of differences in tax and legal systems. And they are ultimately financial, because even prospecting online for customers requires an adequate budget.

That said, the Internet still opens up a wide range of new possibilities to small business. And despite all the media hype about e-tail sales, the greatest short-term potential lies in B2B, particularly in Quebec and Canada. Large (and usually American) distributors are the typical customers of most Canadian small businesses—not individual consumers.

We should also consider the potential of the international B2B market in terms of both export and import. While the Internet is usually associated with new markets, B2B initially served mainly as a way of finding new sources of supply.

The same reasons why big business hopped on board the Internet also apply to small business. While money can be made through Web-based sales, savings can also more easily be realized by cutting supply costs. Ideally, both profits and savings can be produced simultaneously. Online import-export is worth exploring in depth, but a company should give the matter full consideration before taking the plunge. Expert assistance is important, since mistakes can be costly and partial success even more so.

A basis in resources

With the right kind of support, any small business, regardless of size, can take on outside markets. The increasingly numerous prospective partners appearing on the Web can be excellent allies for identifying, seizing and exploiting opportunities—without endangering an existing business. A wealth of Internet-based consultants, governments, start-up ventures and vertical portals on the Internet are encouraging the emergence of global B2B ecommerce.

Governments and public agencies

Governments and public agencies are constantly launching new initiatives to promote the emergence of B2B import-export businesses. Their best-known contributions are Web sites that provide basic information on foreign markets and that make their aid programs known to foreign trade. The first stops, obviously, are Web sites of the various Quebec and federal agencies and organizations responsible for supporting export.

Federal sites include:

- the Department of Foreign Affairs and International Trade (www.maeci.gc.ca),

- Industry Canada's Exportsource (www.exportsource.gc.ca),

- and its huge and essential Strategis database (www.strategis.ic.gc.ca).

On the Quebec side, the Ministère de l'Industrie et du Commerce du Québec (www.micst.gouv.qc.ca/commerce-exterieur/index.html) covers the various trade missions and provides a wealth of information on aid to small business.

U.S. Web sites

A visit to the large export-oriented U.S. Web sites is a must for doing business with the United States.

- Trade Compass (www.tradecompass.com) and Global Sources (www.globalsources.com), for example, offer much advice and provide many leads, addresses, discussion groups and business opportunities.

- The American Society of Association Executives (www.asaenet.org) posts a directory of more than 6,000 U.S. corporations.

- Imarket Inc. (www.imarketinc.com) facilitates market studies by permitting research on virtually any trade sector and also offers business leads.

- More general statistical economic data can be viewed at the U.S. Bureau of Labor Statistics (www.stats.bls.gov) and at the Bureau of Economic Analysis (www.bea.doc.gov).

European sites

- EC Europe (www.eceurope.com) is dedicated exclusively to small business and provides thousands of buyer-seller contacts throughout the European Community.

- The Statistical Office of the European Communities (www.europa.eu.int) publishes data on the European Union.

- Each EU nation also has its own international business assistance bureau. Yahoo! (www.yahoo.com) is the best tool for finding these resources. Links located at the bottom of the Yahoo! home page lead to the portals of some twenty large countries, including France, Sweden, Japan, India, China, and Brazil. These portals in turn connect to national sites containing useful reference information.

- The OECD site (www.oecd.org) offers a wide range of statistics on international business and economic studies of its twenty-nine member nations.

- The International Business Forum (www.ibf.com) provides information on a host of business opportunities throughout the world. It presents business directories of products offered and services sought, for agents and distributors, alliances, marketing networks, as well as a full range of reports and publications.

- The World Chambers Network (www.worldchambers.net) and the Chamber Navigator (www.chambernavigator.com) provide addresses for chambers of commerce around the world.

> Certain governments act directly by creating "business incubators." The Irish Minister of Commerce's Enterprise Ireland has opened offices in New York, Boston, the Silicon Valley and thirty other major cities. The Ministry estimates one Irish company a week has set up shop in the U.S. since early 2000.

Finding the right support

In the case of small business, however, the preferred route to international B2B passes through vertical business portals and the three types of e-marketplaces (neutral, buyers and sellers). Small companies can make ad hoc purchases or establish long-term relationships with suppliers at e-marketplaces regularly visited by different kinds of companies. Sometimes, such opportunities can prove a windfall—like a big discount offered on a part by its overstocked European multinational supplier.

Neutral e-marketplaces

Third parties set up neutral e-marketplaces to bring together buyers and sellers in specialized markets. In most cases, companies register for free and only pay for purchases or sales. However, Mediagrif's Broker Forum[47] charges a yearly fee of $2,000. The most famous neutral e-marketplace is VerticalNet[48]. By late 1999, VerticalNet covered 55 specialized markets in 11 sectors, including communications, automated manufacturing, health, the environment and clothing.

Buyers' e-marketplaces

Buyers' e-marketplaces are B2B portals set up by one or more larger companies to pool their buying power and improve their supply chains. The most famous is Covisint[49], which combines the purchasing power of General Motors, Ford, Chrysler, and Nissan/Renault. The AeroXchange[50] consortium headed by Air Canada merges the buying power of twelve airlines representing 40% of worldwide ticket sales. Sellers' e-marketplaces are aimed at establishing markets controlled by one or more suppliers of goods. Boeing, for instance, hopes to consolidate offers of numerous suppliers for airline products and primarily serve the airline industry.

---

47 www.brokerforum.com
48 www.verticalnet.com
49 www.covisint.com
50 www.aeroxchange.com

Sellers' e-market

By late 2001, the Internet should be under siege from more than a thousand e-marketplaces offering every category of goods and services in all sectors. In fact, at least a half dozen such e-marketplaces have already been announced in every industrial sector. New York's Lehman Brothers brokerage recently listed eight e-marketplaces in the automotive industry (such as covisint.com, istarxhange.com, and fleetworks.com), covering sixteen manufacturers. In the chemical and plastics industry, forty major manufacturers have launched six other e-marketplaces, including chematch.com and elastomersolutions.com. Eight e-marketplaces have taken on thirty-five of the biggest players in the metallurgical sector.

Tricks and tips

Individual small businesses should keep their eyes on any initiatives being made in their respective sectors. It is always worth paying a visit to Vertical Net because of the depth of its coverage. In addition, companies should consult the three big technological suppliers for these e-marketplaces:

• Ariba (www.ariba.com),

• Commerce One (www.commerceone.com) and

• Oracle Systems (www.oracle.com).

Finally, MarketSite (www.marketsite.com) is seeking to establish itself as the reference point for e-marketplaces.

Never quite up to date because of constant evolution in the field, e-marketplace directories have also been set up on Web sites specialized in this area. Net Market Makers'

(NMM) (www.netmarketmakers.com) and B2B Online (http://www.netb2b.com/portalDirectory/index.html) are among the best produced.

A search for "B2B directory" can lead to sites such as b2bYellowPages (www.b2bYellowPages.com), among other links of relative value. While somewhat less useful than the two prior sites, it is nonetheless worth a look.

Logistical and regulatory support

By partnering with a e-marketplace, a small business opens itself to new opportunities. It also avoids the ever-present logistical and regulatory headaches of dealing with foreign partners. In the absence of uniform international legislation, companies should minimize the risk of lawsuits from international buyers or sellers. Firms like the UK's Mesania (www.mesania.com) can help sort through the regulatory maze necessitated by dealing with overseas accounts. Mesania groups small European appliance manufacturers wishing to break into the American market and helps these firms find new customers, get credit, pay customs duties and organize furniture shipments.

Shipping

Shipping is a crucial aspect of any import-export activity. The process may seem too high and too costly a hurdle for a small business making its first ventures abroad. However, value-added shippers offer services such as customs clearance and some have also developed distribution networks for certain markets. In markets where shipping delays are a common headache, it might be worth using the services of a shipper specialized in ecomme rce, such as Oplogistik[51]—the first in its kind in Quebec. A subsidiary of TransForce, this shipper has a warehouse at Mirabel airport where it can store a portion of a customer's stock. Oplogistic can pick a product from a shelf the moment an order is

---

51 www.oplogistik.com

received and handle the entire process of wrapping, same-day shipping by FedEx or UPS and customs formalities.

Payment

The crowning achievement on the road to internationalization is, of course, getting paid. Small businesses can employ all traditional payment methods, including letters of credit and documentary credit collection. Some services now permit online payment when a foreign client purchases industrial products on a regular basis and a certain level of trust exists between the parties.

American Express and Thomas Cook have developed Web-based fund transfer services for commercial partners in different countries. International financial transactions are simplified, while exchange rate risks are minimized.

The importance of being proactive

Whether a small business decides to go it alone or use the services of a e-marketplace in its B2B ecommerce import-export dealings, it must apply procedures inherent in any import-export initiative, with or without an o%nline facet. This means it must conduct a market study, perform fishing expeditions and so forth. But that is not all. Small business must be proactive. It must assign someone who will exploit all promising leads. Over the Web, any company can get an idea of the stability and reliability of a prospective customer with which it has only an email-based relationship. Companies can learn about a prospect's goods or services, while showcasing their own wares on a Web site.

Site promotion

Site promotion is vital not just for consumer-oriented firms, but for industrial concerns as well. This means registering with every possible search engine and online discussion groups, like Global Sources and

EC Europe. Naturally, all traditional forms of publicity, such as foreign tradeshows and advertisements in trade journals must list a corporate Web address. The same goes for all company documents, business cards, wrapping materials and shipping crates.

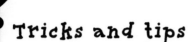

Tricks and tips

Unless a company wants to focus on the U.S. market, international ventures require dealing in a variety of languages. "Netizens" and companies around the world surf the Web in their own tongues. Quebec is one of the few locales where French-speaking Web users may also use English to explore the Internet. It is not always necessary to translate a complete site into the language of the target country. As most business people can read English, a mere site summary in Portuguese, Mandarin or some other language may suffice. The important thing is to be able to draw potential new customers by addressing them in their own language. Once they have arrived at your site, the odds are quite good they will continue to read on in English. But getting them there in the first place requires producing a properly translated summary page to ensure clarity and avoid ambiguity. For example, a product with the name "Nova" might be misunderstood in Spain where "no va" means "doesn't go" or "doesn't work." Having a summary page in a language other than English also lets your site to be indexed by non-English-language search engines.

Beyond language, any small business dealing with a foreign market will benefit from making the many small adjustments that show it is attuned to the customer's cultural sensibilities. This means, for instance, listing prices in target currencies and displaying symbols (like flags or monuments) of the nation with which you are doing business.

The Internet offers a cornucopia of tools and new partners for small businesses seeking to get involved in international ecommerce. But B2B means adopting certain attitudes and procedures that can contribute to success as surely as international prospecting expeditions. This attitude can be summed up as "all or nothing." Satisfaction with half-measures is an invitation to failure. If you have already started investing in B2B, get ready to invest even more!

In brief

- Online import-export is worth exploring in depth, but a company should give the matter full consideration before taking the plunge.

- In the case of small business, the preferred route to international B2B passes through vertical business portals and the three types of e-marketplaces (neutral, buyers and sellers).

- Whether a small business decides to go it alone or use the services of a e-marketplace in its B2B ecommerce import-export dealings, it must be proactive.

PART 3
GETTING
READY

Chapter 11
The Legal Implications of B2B

In collaboration with Normand Gemme

As with any other business, business-to-business e-commerce (B2B) is subject to a set of legal rules and constraints. Despite suggestions to the contrary, B2B is not some sort of electronic free-for-all. Nor, on the other hand, is it a carefully regulated and defined territory where the traditional rules of business apply.

The legal risks inherent in this kind of activity should be carefully weighed before getting involved. Selling products and services from your place of business in Quebec is a relatively simple matter. Opening your shop to the world could, however, mean doing business with undesirable clients or with somewhat less than reliable suppliers. Virtual business transactions can quickly become real nightmares if business owners fail to consider all legal aspects of the situation. This is especially true because the field is new. The rules of the game are quickly evolving—sometimes in unpredictable ways[52].

---

52 We consulted two experts to help us understand these issues. Raymond Picard, a lawyer at Borden Ladner Gervais of Montreal, has specialized in business and corporate law for more than 20 years. Pierre Trudel, a professor at the University of Montreal's Public Law research Centre, is internationally known as an experienced and resourceful cyberlaw specialist.

Rules of the game

A B2B transaction can quickly become a source of potential conflict if the parties to it do not agree on the rules of the game. All B2B business transactions are governed by the usual rules of business—or the rules of common law in lawyers' terms.

Agreement

This means there must be an agreement between both selling and buying parties. In e-commerce transactions, vendors should set down conditions of sale and advise prospective customers of them. Buyers are then responsible for accepting or refusing such terms.

Order or purchase forms are usually available on sites where transactions are performed. These are typically vendor or third-party sites, such as electronic auctions or e-marketplaces, in which customers click to confirm their purchases. The act of clicking signifies that the buyer has agreed to the terms of the contract and both parties have thus agreed to the transaction. The process of purchasing thus appears relatively straightforward.

Litigation

However, any transaction may give rise to disputes or litigation, generally because of assumptions not carefully considered by both parties. A sales contract is legal if it complies with the law in all respects. Are both parties legally entitled to be doing business with each other? Does the vendor or buyer have the required authority to close the deal? Are both signatories of legal age to conclude such agreements? Unsigned sales agreements are still considered by the courts to be binding, if they otherwise meet legal requirements.

Some consider Internet-based sales non-binding because they lack signed contracts. This narrow view fails to consider that a handwritten signature is only one of many legal methods for proving that terms of sale have been accepted. It is not the only kind of admissible legal evidence under this heading, nor is it the only criterion that can validate or nullify a transaction. We shall return to this point later.

E-commerce legislation in Quebec

Since the world of electronics and computers has begun taking a bigger place in the world of business, many countries have revised their legislation to include transactions involving electronic documentation, thereby facilitating the admissibility of non-paper-based documentary evidence. In January 1994, the Government of Quebec enacted a new Civil Code that included legislation pertaining to electronic communications.

Section VI of the Civil Code of Quebec deals with computerized records. Key extracts appear below.

Section 2837

Where the data respecting a juridical act are entered on a computer system, the document reproducing them makes proof of the content of the act if it is intelligible and if its reliability is sufficiently guaranteed.

To assess the quality of the document, the court shall take into account the circumstances under which the data were entered and the document was reproduced.

Section 2838

The reliability of the entry of the data of a juridical act on a computer system is presumed to be sufficiently guaranteed where it is carried out systematically and without gaps and the computerized data are protected against alterations. The same presumption is made in favour of third persons where the data were entered by an enterprise.

Section 2839

A document which reproduces the data of a computerized juridical act may be contested on any grounds.

These three sections make it clear that information from a legal document in an electronic format may be presented in evidence so long as the data is reliable—but that it may, however, also be contested.

Federal E-commerce legislation

The federal government recently enacted Bill C-6 in support of e-commerce. The law defines the concepts of *electronic signature* and *electronic document.* It provides that electronic signatures are legal and valid means for approving e-commerce sales. This law allowed the federal government to fill a legal void in this area—electronic transactions can now be submitted as legal evidence. The Canadian legislation was based on a generic e-commerce signature model that had been adopted by the United Nations. This fact boosts the likelihood that Canadian law will correspond with similar laws in many countries, helping reduce confusion and uncertainties in international transactions.

Federal law also protects electronically gathered personal information. However, federal law has no jurisdiction over commercial matters in Quebec, so the Civil Code usually applies to matters falling within its scope.

Quebec legal normalization bill

The Government of Quebec hopes to draw on federal law to enact its own rules on legal standardization of new information technologies. Such a draft bill has been submitted to the Quebec National Assembly, which is expected to approve it in 2001.

The new law goes into greater detail on certain issues pertaining to the legal security of communications provided in real or virtual documents than does Quebec's Civil Code, as amended in 1994. It stipulates that a "reliable document" has full legal value and sets out applicable rules of proof. The draft legislation released to the public recognizes the possibility of using various means of authenticating parties communicating through electronic documents.

Transactions lacking handwritten signatures

Verbal agreement

E-commerce transactions resemble telephone transactions in certain respects. Case law accepts verbal agreements between the parties as binding in such cases.

E-commerce transactions are also similar to those conducted by fax. Electronically transmitted documents have had legal authority since the 1994 amended Civil Code, and may be produced as evidence in court.

Electronic signature

Certain acts of sale require handwritten signatures, as in the case of contracts that must be notarized. Electronic signatures will be imperative for this kind of situation. These signatures take the form of a message containing a series of encrypted letters and numbers produced by software designed for that specific purpose. Only the originator knows the message and the encryption code. This method can be used cheaply and effectively if recognized by the courts in the country in which such a transaction takes place[53].

There are no borders on the Internet

Predicted in 1962 by Canadian Marshall McLuhan, the global village came into its own on the Internet—a magnificent tool for bringing

---

53 Legislation in Quebec and Canada is described above.

together the world's peoples on a single network. The Internet gives new meaning and unheralded assistance to the process of globalization. In theory, ecommerce is available to anyone who takes the trouble to sell products or services ove r the Web.

People who are thousands of kilometres apart can be quickly and easily reached over the Internet. No barriers prevent a company from buying goods over the Internet from sellers on the other side of the globe. Why not, for example, get hotel reservations over the Web for a convention in Arizona? On the other hand, maybe your company has purchased software and you are not satisfied. Problems will begin to arise when you consider suing the supplier.

Which laws apply?

The question of conflict of laws does not apply if you are doing e-commerce with companies within Quebec, as both parties are governed by the same legal system. The situation is hazier when transactions occur between companies operating in different countries. Which legal system will settle eventual conflicts? The answer is not an easy one.

Tricks and tips

Legal advisors recommend specifying in the sales contract which laws and jurisdictions will govern in the event of a dispute.

In certain cases, sales contracts may require international rules of arbitration or laws adopted by the United Nations that would prevail over local legislation.

Where did the transaction take place?

When transactions occur over the telephone, many courts in Quebec, as well as in several American states, have ruled a transaction takes place where a call is received. This means the governing law would be that of the seller.

On the other hand, when a company operates a Web site accessed from another country, many American courts have ruled this is like having a place of business in the territory from which the site was accessed. For Web-based transactions involving American companies, laws of the customer's jurisdiction usually apply. OECD guidelines recommend universal adoption of the same principle. However, it would make sense for the time being to see what rules apply in the country with which you are doing business.

A company is best served by stipulating the applicable jurisdiction in the sales contract. Case costs will be very high if you have to travel overseas for litigation in France or Italy, for example. It is best to prepare for this type of situation in advance.

Data security

E-commerce transactions are often paid by credit card, another potential source of legal conflict.

This means purchasers must reveal confidential information, such as credit card numbers, opening the door to possible fraud. Data is not always secure and customers do not know who has access to such information, which can be intercepted by cybercriminals.

The confidentiality of commercial and personal data must also be considered.

Tricks and tips

The manner in which this information will be used must be clearly stated in a policy (a privacy statement), which usually appears on any responsible company's Website. Many sales contracts explicitly stipulate liability limits in this area.

Rights and prerogatives

Laws and agreements protecting certain rights may complicate matters, especially in international transactions involving copyrights, patents, trademarks and so forth.

Protecting territories

In ordinary business, many companies strike up commercial alliances with partners to share sales territory. The Internet however operates without borders. Customers can place orders to any online nation on seven continents.

It is harder to protect commercial territory when orders are coming in from around the world. A company, for instance, may decide to sell online without bothering to consider exclusive deals with distributors to certain provinces, state or countries. Customers opting to bypass the distributor and deal directly with the head office over the Internet could infringe on such exclusivity. Any litigation under this heading would, however, affect the seller and the distributor—not the buyer.

A company's computer specialists—who may fail to consider the issue of exclusive territory—are often the ones who develop online and electronic sales services.

Managing brand names

The process of managing and protecting brand names presents another kind of problem. Certain companies have registered trademarks for which they hold exclusive rights of sale for a well-defined territory. A company's right to sell a product could be severely limited in a territory reserved for another seller.

A trademark may be reserved for one company in one country and for another company somewhere else. Ownership of domain names generally complies with rules governing trademarks, but the situation as a whole remains unsettled.

Copyright

Copyright concerns are also important in electronic commerce. Software is one of the products most sold over the Web and is protected by copyright. When a software purchase involves two different countries, should the customer pay royalties? The typical American "shrink-wrap" agreement stating that the act of opening a package implies the purchaser's acceptance of sales conditions and terms of use is meeting resistance in some countries. Applicable regulations must be clearly posted on transaction sites.

Problem countries

A Quebec-based concern should think twice about doing business with a company located in a nation with a poor business reputation. A company based in a country with poorly defined or barely applied rules of commerce can become a major cause of headaches.

Certain African and South American countries have been sources of problems in the past. For example, laws are not applied as rigorously in Nigeria as they are in Quebec. A seller's rights might not be recognized for products purchased in Quebec and later sold in Nigeria. Company management should be advised if the sales department decides to sell in Nigeria. This type of situation—including the increased difficulty of proving facts in foreign courts of law—is not exclusive to e-commerce but is likely to crop up with increasing frequency as e-commerce proliferates.

Conversion of the Canadian dollar into foreign currency is another source of potential trouble. Not only must exchange rates be determined, but restrictions on the free flow of money from the purchaser's country should be considered. A number of countries have currency exchange controls that may pose problems to international trade.

Certification for high risk

Individual purchases of inexpensive goods may not carry much risk, as risk varies in proportion to the cost and value of goods concerned. Consequently, when it comes to high value items, parties will want to be certain of the identities and business capacities of the parties with which they are dealing. This is where certification come in. Certification services help ensure that a particular electronic signature belongs to the intended party to the transaction.

The Quebec registre des droits personnels et réels mobiliers (Register of Personal and Movable Rights—RDPRM)

The RDPRM is an organization that has created a register of goods on which rights or liens are held by parties other than their owners. It is the first Quebec-based group to systematically apply the certification process to validate identities of individuals or organizations. The register is available over the Internet and can be used to determine if a corporation's assets are registered with it, thereby severely limiting an owner's ability to dispose of such property. For instance, the register states if a financial institution has claims on certain goods. This electronic tool can prevent transactions with parties that are not lawful owners of the property they are selling.

RPMRR information is highly secure, because all individuals and corporations must use third-party certificates to validate their signatures. Because of such tools, no party can pass itself off for another and make false claims on property.

The legal audit

In order to assess the risks of e-commerce better, a transaction site can be assessed through what is termed a "legal audit." Performed by a specialist, this process involves a comprehensive analysis of a company's Web site prior to the launch of e-commerce operations. The practice is strongly recommended for big transactions or for establishing long-term relationships with trading partners.

This type of assessment makes it possible to review all commercial operations before they occur, by identifying prospective trading partners, determining where they are based in the world and estimating all potential legal risks before starting operations. An audit will focus on all prospective conflicts and determine which jurisdictions would apply. A legal audit will also determine the company's position under legislation pertaining, for example, to regulated products such as medication.

These audits are performed in Quebec by specialized firms of accountants or lawyers. Audits also serve to identify pertinent legislation for any sites aimed at minors, as well as determine if existing advertising complies with the law. Experts all agree on one point. The more a company does business over the Internet, the more risks it must manage.

Despite the many problems enumerated in this section, we can conclude on a reassuring note. Commercial sites that comply with European and American laws are usually in line with most international legal systems as well.

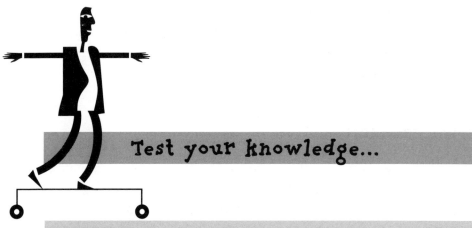

Test your knowledge...

True or False?

E-marketplaces redefine the relationship between buyers and sellers by optimizing the value added chain, starting with the elimination of unnecessary processes.

1. True

2. False

3. Neither True nor False
   (Answer p. 59)

Each contributor to the chain strengthens his position in proportion to the value he adds to the product.

1. True

2. False

3. Neither True nor False
   (Answer p. 30)

Small businesses and independent contractors are the principal users targeted by B2B e-commerce.

1. True

2. False

3. Neither True nor False
   (Answer p. 17)

To stand out from the competition in B2B, the sector that has become the most strategic is no longer security, nor online payment, but logistics (on-time delivery.)

1. True
2. False
3. Neither True nor False
   (Answer p. 120)

If you'd like to learn more...

Sections from the Civil Code of Quebec

http://www.lexum.umontreal.ca/ccq/en/l7/t2/c1/s6/2837a2839.html

Bill C-6 adopted by the House of Commons on October 26, 1999

http://www.parl.gc.ca/36/2/parlbus/chambus/house/bills/government/C-6/C-6_3/90052b-3E.html

Draft Bill: An Act respecting the legal normalization of new information technologies.

http://www.assnat.qc.ca/eng/publications/av-projets/00-aap01.htm

In brief

- All B2B business transactions are governed by the usual rules of business—or the rules of common law in lawyers' terms.

- The federal government recently enacted Bill C-6 in support of e-commerce. The law defines the concepts of electronic signature and electronic document. It provides that electronic signatures are legal and valid means for approving e-commerce sales.

- Legal advisors recommend putting in the sales contract which laws and jurisdictions will govern in the event of a dispute.

- Commercial sites that comply with European and American laws are usually in line with most international legal systems as well.

CHAPTER 12
SECURITY: THE CRITICAL FACTOR

In collaboration with Renato Cudicio

Many companies have placed their e-commerce activities on the back burner because of Internet security concerns. There is some justification for such hesitation. The Computer Security Institute estimates financial losses from 1999 break-ins into the networks of large American organizations doubled in relationship to average annual losses for the period 1996 through 1998.

While no business should let down its guard, certain facts should be kept in mind. Eighty percent of corporate data is of no interest to anyone but the intended recipient. The biggest security holes result from security policies that are lax or are poorly communicated to employees. Employees usually cause twice the security problems created by outsiders. While not all hackers have malicious intentions, most are interested in hacking their way into the higher profile and more challenging systems.

With the right priorities in place and backed by properly deployed technology, the risk of network break-ins is comparable to the risk of off-line attacks. Despite the possibility of fraud, credit card companies and banks are constantly offering an increasing number of online services. Business in general should learn to offset increased risk with increased efficiency. When losses do occur, they should be assumed as part of the cost of doing business.

Of course, the better you understand the tools, the better you can use them. In this chapter, we will review the main aspects of security and the tools for applying them: firewalls, encrypted communications, authentication and certification.

Piracy and viruses

In 1983, the film War Games alerted the world to the dangers of computer piracy. Eleven years later, the business community was shocked to see life reflecting art. In 1994, the New York network of a Citibank affiliate was broken into by a hacker in Saint Petersburg, Russia, who managed to transfer $11 million U.S. to three personal bank accounts in Finland, Israel, and California.

This spectacular event made the security of commercial Internet activities a top concern for information system managers in both big and small companies. Over time, techniques have improved and the number of security tools has increased. Some large firms now specialize in the very lucrative market of computer security. Nonetheless, a threat to companies of every shape or size persists.

Particularly nasty computer viruses and booby-trapped software are spreading like wildfire on the Net. The lack of standards and the NSA (National Security Administration) prohibition on export of high-encryption algorithms outside the U.S., the lack of political will in Washington and elsewhere and the many managers with their heads in the sand are some of the reasons for this spreading phenomenon . Putting security policies into place requires very strict discipline on the parts of company employees and perfect coordination of equipment, software and security protocols. This is why more and more companies are integrating security into their operational processes and software tools.

Is it possible to unify procedures and comprehensively protect a network in an era of virtual private networks (VPN), telecommuting, virtual companies and telecollaboration? Keeping information secure is a fairly new and difficult art that requires special care. We must also bear in mind that security is a concept and not a software application or piece of equipment.

Tricks and tips

While most company information does not really need to be secure, correct identification of what does require secure treatment is important. The best way to start determining security requirements is by classifying equipment, software and data by their relative degrees of confidentiality or risk. The Orange Book published by the American Defense Department lists seven security levels, ranging from "A1" for systems based on complex mathematical models protecting top secret information to "D" for unsecured systems. Subsequently adopted by the TCSEC (Trusted Computer System Evaluation Criteria), business can apply these definitions to setting up an excellent set of security procedures.

B2B versus B2C security

Security on the Internet is a hazy concept. We should distinguish between the security constraints peculiar to B2B e-commerce and those security problems particular to business-to-consumer (B2C) trade over the Internet, as the latter has drawn far more media attention.

B2B e-commerce is a concept covering a host of commercial activities ranging from EDI and knowledge sharing to the sending and receiving of email. Online B2C payments mainly involve transmission of credit card numbers over secure links to pay for goods or services. Because so many Netizens make online payments, this issue naturally generates a lot of literature, studies and software applications, all of which are aimed at reassuring those involved in this kind of trade.

It is, however, B2B transactions that make up the lion's share of Internet-based business transactions and deserve special attention. Fifty-four percent of all hacking incidents were routed over the Internet, according to a 1998 Computer Security Institute and FBI Computer Crimes Department survey of 520 systems security administrators. With the rapid proliferation of TCP/IP protocols, open architectures, telecommuting and online file sharing—which make up the toolkits of all modern and competitive companies—businesses have permitted wide breaches in their security systems. The problem is compounded by less-than-rigourous validation of system users and the failure to quickly patch leaks when problems arise.

The three faces of security

There are three types of computer security: physical security, passive security and active network security, all of which can be combined with anti-virus protection.

Physical security

Physical network security has long been a topic of debate among computer security specialists. A stolen diskette, an illicit copy of a file and internal access permitted by a negligent employee present the greatest risks and represent the most common kinds of computer crime.

Passive security

Passive security is the most popular approach, involving firewalls, encryption software, public/private keys, password systems and control systems of varying degrees of complexity. Canadian companies spent nearly $1 billion for such systems in 1999, according to Dataquest. American companies spent nearly $12 billion U.S. over the same period. Strong growth in the security software market is reassuring evidence that business information system specialists are aware of the hazards of the Internet. It is also an indication that these same specialists may occasionally rely too heavily on such systems to protect their operations.

Active security

Just as preventing shoplifting requires constant vigilance and alert employees, protecting data moving through a network or stored on a server requires readiness combined with intelligent systems able to detect abnormal situations. This process is called active security.

Active security requires systems that maintain a constant watch over network activity. Called "IDS" for Intrusion Detection Systems, they are connected like bank security systems to security centres where experts maintain a constant vigil, analyzing and interpreting abnormal corporate network data in real time.

Active security is enjoying strong growth in the United States and will soon spread throughout the industrialized world. The concept is presently available in Quebec and Canada at rates permitting small business to put such remote surveillance of networks in the hands of specialists.

> *Computer World* magazine speaks of an annual 100% growth in this sector, estimated at $100 million CND in 2000. This shows the amounts now being spent are far too little. What is the point of installing an armour-plated door if we have no way of knowing if someone is actually trying to get in—or, worse, is already inside?

Anyone well informed in the security field realizes that few small businesses are likely to transform themselves into virtual Fort Knoxes. An overview of tools used by serious computer security specialists will provide a broader and more balanced view of the issue. The main security tools are firewalls, encrypted communications and authentication through digital signatures.

Firewalls

The firewall is clearly the first line of defence against hackers in both passive and active systems. Firewalls maintain a constant watch over data circulating on a server, while filtering access to it.

We should remember that computers connected to the Internet use the TCP/IP protocol to talk with other email servers, the Web, etc. One or more server ports is assigned to each function, as each port acts as a channel of communications between the computer and the network.

Not all ports are constantly in use and inactive ports can serve as pathways into a computer. Hacker "robots" search the Internet looking for open and inactive ports. When one is found, a hacker can break into a computer and install a "Trojan horse" like the infamous Back Orifice. Hackers can then take effective control of a server—with all the consequences that implies.

Cost

A wide diversity of firewalls can block or filter access to such breaches. Prices range from $50 for personal firewalls to nearly $10,000 for sophisticated systems that permit remote management and incorporate a full set of security protocols. Each kind of system is a compromise between data processing speed and security. Any company requiring top security must learn to live with such protocols and accept reduced access speeds.

IDS

Intrusion Detection Systems (IDS) are extensions of the firewall principle. They can remotely monitor and analyze in real time unknown signatures, suspicious movements, excessively large or systematic data transfers, repeated attempts to obtain access codes or even Web surfing styles that trigger alarms. When an alert occurs, the IDS sends email to the system administrator, blocks access to the network and will even cut power to the server, if necessary.

Figure 8   Security

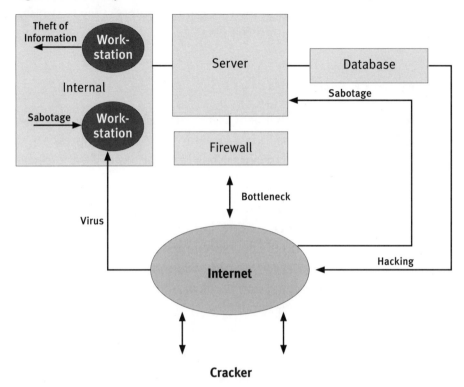

The Internet has facilitated a proliferation in security issues.

Encrypted digital communications

Grasping the importance of using data encryption software to secure the transmission of confidential messages over the Internet requires an understanding of how Internet-based communications are structured, and is at the root of all public network security issues.

Different levels

Computer networks consist of three levels:

- Software (Web browsers, email software, and operating systems)
- Communications (Internet TCP/IP protocols used to transmit messages)

- Network (home of the more primitive protocols as well as all electronic system components, such as cables, routers, switches, hubs, gateways, etc. needed to transmit data).

Information transfer

Information is always exchanged asynchronously over the Internet, although high-speed connections sometimes give the impression of simultaneity. Asynchronous transmission can facilitate illicit message interception.

The process starts when a user enters data into a browser. When transmission occurs, a sender's and recipient's address and other technical parameters are added to the encrypted message. This additional data permits Internet protocols to perform addressing and routing tasks. Finally, the message is entered into the flow of data along the route and electronic equipment assigned to it.

Once the destination is reached, the message is decrypted. It is "unwrapped" from the network level to a communication level where it is once more unwrapped to a software level so it can be read by its intended recipient. Technically, the whole process requires seven, rather than three, stages. Security can obviously be breached at each level and every time a message is enriched with new content. Furthermore, every process on this very public network takes place in plain view. This means content can easily be read by the average hacker.

The four basic security concepts

We depend on four basic security concepts to prevent hacking and break-ins.

- Confidentiality (no one except the intended recipient can read a message)
- Authentication (to guarantee sender and recipient identities)

- Data integrity (the recipient is sure no one has read or corrupted the message)

- Non-repudiation (provides proof the recipient has received the message).

Each of these operations should be secured with the appropriate software and equipment without overtaxing system management or impeding the data transaction process.

Authentication and certification

As much as we may wish for perfectly secure e-commerce transactions, this will not happen. Too many parties are involved between the sender and recipient to totally control this situation, even if a communication is merely from one street corner to the next. That is why technology for encrypting data and for authenticating e-signatures has become essential, if not to initiate a B2B transaction, then at least to permit close cooperation on highly confidential projects.

Figure 9   Authentification

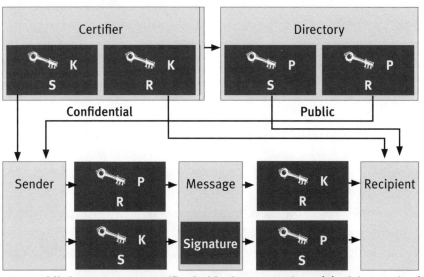

In a public key system, a certifier holds the secrets keys (K) of the sender (S) and recipient (R) and publishes their public keys (P) in an open directory.

Symmetric encryption

If we want to be sure information is meaningless to all except intended recipients—who will receive it in an unaltered and authenticated form—we must use encryption and electronic signatures. Until recently, this meant using symmetric encryption technology, which requires use of a secret key. A secret key permits encryption and decryption of messages, which are authenticated by virtue of their decryption. IBM's DES (Data Encryption Standard) algorithm, used mainly by banks to protect transaction details, is one example of this approach.

This system has one major drawback, however. It requires the sender and the recipient use the same key, which must be exchanged offline for greater security. The key's inviolability depends on the method used to transmit it and the number of randomly generated digits used to create it.

Asymmetric cryptography

The communications security field is now being revitalized through application of a new technique—asymmetric cryptography. Officially discovered in the 1970s by three MIT professors, it perfectly fills the need for encrypting strategic data transmitted over the Internet. Asymmetric cryptography uses a dual (public and private) key system. Both keys are generated using advanced mathematical formulas. The main advantage of asymmetric cryptography is that it eliminates the need to exchange secret keys.

This means we can deal securely over the Internet with a third party without knowing or having access to its secret encryption key. Asymmetric cryptography makes it possible to transmit encrypted messages that can only then be decrypted with the recipient's private key and the sender's public key. Both keys must be issued by a certification body that maintains an up-to-date directory of public keys. Any interested party can look up another party's public key to decrypt and authenticate a confidential message or to send that party a message.

This technology is now available to small business thanks to banks and other players who have become interested in offering certification services to businesses. As senders and recipients do not usually share the same certification services, certification service providers will form a "public key infrastructure" (PKI) to enable such services to communicate with each other. A PKI is a hierarchical structure where national proxies in each country are authorized to authenticate national key holders to foreign recipients, represented in turn by their own national certification services.

> The largest project of this type in Canada is taking place in the Province of Ontario. The Canadian subsidiary of Entrust Technologies has been asked to set up a public key broadcast infrastructure to secure data transfers between Ontario's government employees. The service will eventually be extended to the Province's eleven million residents so they can communicate with the Ontario government.

Biometrics

Most of the time, asymmetric cryptography is sufficiently secure for communications with outside parties. It is inadequate, however, when the transactions and stakes are high and require great confidentiality. Large bank transfers, remote management of security systems, patent consultation and sensitive databases are some examples. In such cases, the most effective method is biometrics. Until very recently, computer terminals were linked to fingerprint readers or voice recognition systems. The authenticity of a given party can be adequately assured when biometrics are used in conjunction with a public/private key system and encryption software.

Iris recognition

State-of-the-art security systems today are built around iris recognition systems. The iris of the eye has hundreds of identification points, while fingerprints have only a few dozen. This personal ID card—there are no two on Earth alike—is impossible to steal unless someone is taken hostage. Moreover, it is even more difficult than fingerprints to fake. In the future, it should serve as the best identification tool for highly secure processes.

If you'd like to learn more...

Visit Internet/Network Security, a comprehensive site that describes security issues related to the digital economy in plain language.
http://www.netsecurity.about.com/compute/netsecurity/mbody.htm

Read: Best Practices in Network Security, an article by Network Computing, published in March 2000 and summarizing the best electronic communications security practices.
http://www.networkcomputing.com/1105/1105f2.html

Visit CERT/CC (Computer Emergency Response Team Coordination Center) a centre of Internet security expertise set up by the Software Engineering Institute of Carnegie Mellon University in the U.S., under the auspices of DARPA (Defense Advanced Research Projects Agency), a U.S. Defense agency supporting technological research.
http://www.cert.org/

Read the summary of Les enjeux du marché de la sécurité des systèmes d'information en France. Bilan et Perspectives 1998-2002 : Le marché français des produits et services associés, a study conducted by IDG France, French subsidiary of an American firm conducting research on technological trends.
http://www.idc.fr/etudes/securite.htm

In brief

- Business in general should learn to offset increased risk with increased efficiency. When losses do occur, they should be assumed as part of the cost of doing business.

- Protecting data moving through a network or stored on a server requires readiness combined with intelligent systems able to detect abnormal situations.

- Any company requiring top security must learn to live with such protocols and accept reduced access speeds.

CHAPTER 13
IMPLEMENTATION

We are likely never to find a single model for B2B e-commerce that will serve the ends of all small businesses. Not only does a different situation apply to each industry, but to each industrial sector, based on a company's size and the role it plays within the value chain. Furthermore, it would be highly speculative to make any universal predictions while this new way of doing business is still in its infancy.

In five or ten years the case may change, but at the current time not every business requires a transactional Web site to participate in the B2B economy. Before a company decides to take on the world through B2B, it should make sure its own house is in order—and start by implementing email as a means of streamlining business with key customers. If a company wants to break into the U.S. market, it will probably attract more attention by its presence on one or two appropriate American B2B e-marketplaces than with a medium-sized Web site.

In contrast with the currents of 1998 and 1999, the rise of the digital economy, which had become a fact of life by 2000, lost some of its glimmer following the nose-dive in dot-com stocks that year. The turnaround means conventional enterprises will be under less pressure to mindlessly leap onto the B2B bandwagon—or to fail to take the time to review any errors made once adopting this course.

While established companies have gained more time to better digest the various stages involved in their respective commitments to B2B e-commerce, they should be wary of excessive delay. The burst in the bubble of Internet company share prices forced start-up concerns to take stock of the situation and settle for more conventional ways of doing business. However solidly established businesses should never for a moment consider putting off the migration of their business communications to the Internet.

This chapter serves as a guide to today's online contenders to the extent possible, since few examples of small businesses seriously committed to B2B e-commerce had come to light by the fall of 2000. Lacking any proven formulas applicable to business as a whole, we shall discuss some measures that can be adopted and whether or not they are universally acceptable.

Exaggerated risk of the status quo

Before starting our review of the various phases involved in B2B e-commerce, we should put into perspective the widespread panic created by hi-tech suppliers intent on selling their wares. While the current revolution is real and will sooner or later affect all small businesses, there is no cause for alarm about the need to catch up with American small businesses.

> While most major Canadian companies are taking far longer to move online than their American counterparts, the proportion of Quebec- and Canadian-based small businesses using the Internet was quite similar to that of American firms in the summer of 2000. According to a survey of the Canadian Federation of Independent Business, 77% of Canadian companies with 20 to 49 employees were already online. This figure climbed to 82% for companies with 50 to 99 employees. An Arthur Andersen survey released at the same time revealed 85% of American small businesses were using the Internet. The gap was greater, however, when it came to more sophisticated usage, as only 21% of Canadian small businesses had company Web sites as opposed to 33% of American small businesses.

Nonetheless, companies should refrain from going overboard in this area, as technology is fast evolving, products better adapted to the needs of small business have just arrived on the market and the volume of B2B transactions—compared with the total number of offline transactions between businesses—is still minuscule. According to a survey of the U.S. National Association of Manufacturers, more than two thirds of all American manufacturers had not yet conducted any B2B e-commerce as of mid-2000. Various sources put the number of B2B ecommerce transactions in the U.S. at between 1% and 5% of the total number of B2B exchanges.

Our difficulty in finding—even in the U.S.—any meaningful examples of B2B e-commerce applications by small business shows how far this new form of business has to go before it is accepted as a standard. B2B e-marketplaces, covering needs of vertical industries like the agri-food business, or providing horizontal services aimed at small business as a whole, have failed to provide the names of any participating small businesses—although they claim to have thousands of members.

In view of these results, Quebec- and Canada-based small businesses can remain at ease. If they move quickly to launch into B2B e-commerce activities, they should be able to catch up with their American competitors caught in the grips of a situation very much like their own. A primer on the five basic steps to B2B is provided below.

Step 1: Field reconnaissance

Companies that have steered clear of the Internet, or have used it only minimally, should begin by becoming better acquainted with this medium if they want to use it as a means of setting themselves apart from the competition in their fields. But they should first devote some time to exploring its various possibilities.

This exploratory phase means assigning one or more persons, depending on available resources, to visit a range of Web sites within the industry, learn what the competition is doing, join discussion groups in various forums—like marketing, export and technologies, identify potentially useful vertical and horizontal e-marketplaces, and so forth. Unless a company already has Web-literate employees, this task should be assigned to those in charge of marketing, R&D, competitive intelligence and so forth.

This first step will help a company acquire Internet experience that can be put to good use to better plan the following stages when the time comes for considering a deeper commitment.

Step 2: Strategic thinking

Once a company is ready to pursue this tack, it should conduct a detailed strategic analysis based on market position and financial means before making serious preparations. This phase requires the appointment of a project supervisor to coordinate the human and technical resources necessary to carry out the plan.

In this case, as in all others where business practices could be affected, project success is directly linked to the involvement of senior management. Since taking the plunge into the world of B2B is likely to have a long-term impact on the way a company does business, management should carefully map out the process. In particular, it should make sure business needs take priority over technological considerations—and never the reverse. All details of overseeing this job on a day-to-day basis should be the responsibility of the project manager, who should in turn report directly to the company's head or one of the latter's senior aides.

The company must from the start review its fundamentals to produce an ideal overview of the right path to take. It should bear in mind these fundamentals must also sustain its online business strategy. The strengths and weaknesses of its fundamentals should be reviewed and compared with those of competitors. The company should also produce a representative portrait of its customer base, along with a precise description of the ways its B2B project is likely to bolster customer loyalty.

Step 3: Master plan

Once this strategic review has been completed, the company should have a clear idea of how it can distinguish itself in B2B e-commerce. It will then be able to produce a master plan, yielding clear and assessable objectives.

Appropriate goals will vary, depending on the company's existing market position and the new profile it hopes to achieve by adopting B2B to deal with suppliers, partners and customers. One strategy might be to streamline upstream transactions with its partners. Another might be to enhance downstream business with its customers.

Here are a few examples of possible goals:

- Raise profits by slashing overhead.
- Increase business by seeking new customers and new markets.
- Cut customer service calls by posting FAQs (frequently-asked questions) on the company's Web site.

Tricks and tips

Companies should not try to do too much too soon. They should set priorities based on precise and easily measurable objectives, so they can determine returns on investment and then fine-tune their efforts down the line. Companies should also be aware that, while industry-wide innovations could ultimately change the shape of their industries, a small business should never set out on such a task alone.

Big improvements can be achieved with small changes. A company can considerably cut incoming phone calls, for example, by posting a list of FAQs to its Web site, as mentioned above, and guiding customers to that site when they phone up for information.

All master plans should provide for the retraining of employees, as their tasks will change when the company begins doing B2B ecommerce. If a company plans to sell its products or services directly over its Web site, itr should obviously rally all employees behind the effort—starting with sales reps who will likely be transformed into customer service consultants.

Step 4: Planning the deployment

Once a company's goals have been set out, it must select the best means of achieving them. The scope of a company's commitment, its budget and its internal resources will result in various approaches to the following six points.

- Type of content to be developed: basic information on the company, its products, its distributors, an online catalogue if appropriate, inventory databases, order follow-up, along with the decision to provide such information to customers, suppliers and partners.

- Procedures to be optimized: the company will be in a position to determine which procedures should be automated, starting with tasks that produce paperwork and no added value.

- The right partnerships: a company may want to entrust the production of its Web site to a communications agency, and the development of a secure transactional site to experts in that field.

- The marketing plan: a share of the budget should be applied to promoting the company site and updating company brochures, business cards, letterheads and so forth to include the new company Web site and email addresses.

- Customer involvement: to obtain a swift return on investment, customers should be steered to the site and given the email addresses of their company contacts.

- Outsourcing: to make up for any lack of company skills in the area, the site should be hosted by an Internet access provider to ensure it is always accessible.

The company should also seek advice from consultants, or at least from other companies that have already gone through this process, on each of these items.

Step 5: Development

Analysis

Before committing itself to any expenditures, company management should review both the master plan and means of achieving it, to avoid two common pitfalls. The project should fit into the company's overall strategies and streamline current procedures, rather than merely add a virtual dimension to them. The company should also maintain overall control of the project and resist grandiose offers from suppliers proposing turnkey systems to "meet all needs." More often than not, such solutions include built-in constraints that make it very difficult to subsequently modify a site—even though changes are almost always necessary.

Third Party Hosting

A company that decides to host its site with a third party should check into the solvency of the selected supplier and the latter's ability to support the various technologies employed. The company should find out exactly how updates will be made, make sure bandwidth is adequate so pages load quickly, learn about accessing site statistics and so forth.

Graphics

Whether the company develops its own site or outsources the task, it should keep its graphic artists, who often tend to go overboard, in check. In B2B e-commerce, the key to success is site effectiveness and user friendliness. Commercial customers tend to be far less impressed than consumers with a site's bells and whistles. They are usually most concerned with the quality of services offered.

Content

For this same reason, the site should avoid the commercial hype of advertising brochures. Objective information that gets straight to the point will yield a better impression than bold claims. Credibility is crucial, since the competition is just a mouse click away. A company seeking to draw new customers to its Web site will want to make sure it is believable.

Step 6: Going online

Testing

A site should be tested—and retested—before it goes online. A variety of bugs plague most new sites and links often lead nowhere. To avoid these drawbacks, which can annoy visitors or totally turn them off, find representatives from your target audience who will help test it out.

Marketing

Before launching your site, you should conduct a promotional campaign among prospective users through both conventional and Internet-based marketing methods. Direct marketing yields the best results in B2B e-commerce, because the prospective audience is often a limited one.

Evaluation

Site traffic should be analyzed shortly after the launch to determine if the company's new goals appear attainable. If not, perhaps they were set too high.

Improvement

Even if a company is upbeat about results, it should work from the start to eliminate any weak points. Every Web site should be fine-tuned from the moment it goes online. The best sites undergo a wide number of modifications the first year. As with consumer-oriented sites, B2B sites should remain under periodic review and reconstruction for several years.

If you'd like to learn more...

Visit the site of the Electronic Commerce Institute, a non-profit organization serving to encourage the adoption of e-business by Quebec-based companies in general and small businesses in particular.
http://www.institut.qc.ca

Read The B2B Internet Report-Collaborative Commerce, a report by analysts Chuck Phillips and Mary Meeker from Morgan Stanley Dean Witter.
http://www.msdw.com/institutional/eInterpriseSoftware/194.html

In brief

- If Quebec- and Canada-based small businesses move quickly to launch into B2B e-commerce activities, they should be able to catch up with their American competitors caught in the grips of a situation very much like their own.

- Project success is directly linked to the involvement of senior management.

- Priorities set should be based on precise and easily measurable objectives so returns on investment can be determined and efforts fine-tuned down the line.

CONCLUSION
COLLABORATING TO THE NTH DEGREE

At the dawn of the twenty-first century, it is virtually impossible to choose a universal approach that can be applied by all small businesses to B2B e-commerce. Business models and strategies designed to make a particular enterprise stand out from the competition vary from company to company.

Some facts, however, are increasingly clear. The biggest gains of business will come not from automated transactions, but from enhanced efficiency through better collaboration among companies—both before and after they conclude their transactions. Although this trend has long been predicted, the software needed to meet this need was sorely lacking until mid-2000.

The computer industry, well known for dreaming up new labels for existing technologies purely for purposes of marketing, practically fell over itself endorsing the Gartner Group's term ccommerce, in which the "c" for "ecollaborative commerce" has come to replace the "e" for "electronic commerce," as the most appropriate identifier for sophisticated B2B e-commerce functions. For once, the change was more than just hype.

This new B2B concept reflects the industry's acknowledgement that it is difficult to completely automate business-to-business exchanges and that it might preferable to retain a fair share of human intervention. Such a conclusion is no surprise. Companies will probably never be able to relegate the task of creating and maintaining the chemistry needed for positive long-term relationships between partners.

Figure 10   Collaboration in the construction industry

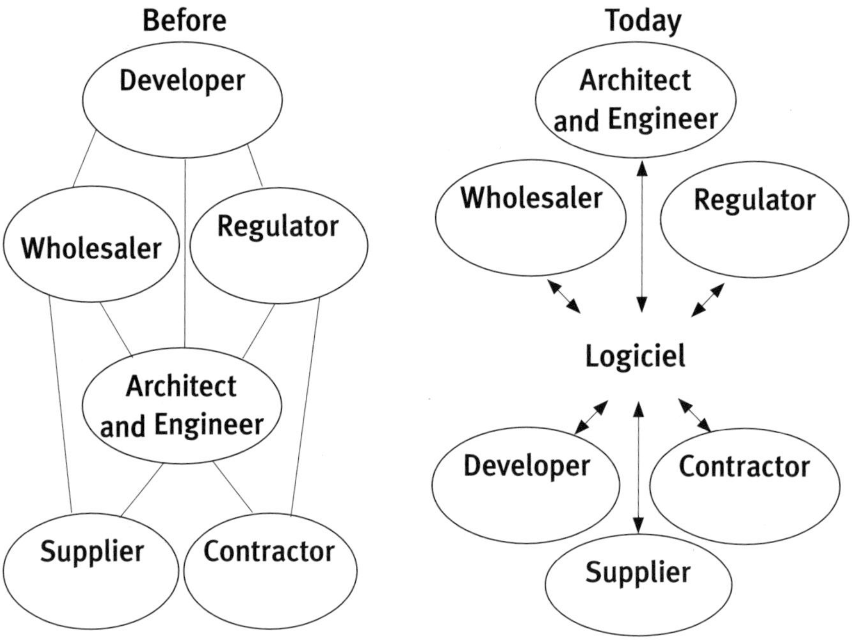

With the Internet, multiple actors in a construction project can share the same work.

No future for ordinary intermediaries

Targeting of narrower niches, just-in-time shipments, vanishing inventories, one-to-one marketing and optimized chains of logistics are all viewed as legitimate goals by many company directors—and this is just as well. Thanks to the Internet, these leading-edge strategies will eventually impose themselves as essentials for remaining in business.

The Internet's ability to help data flow more swiftly both within and outside a business can be applied to the process of quickly revamping not only internal business procedures, but those at each link in a value-added chain involving partners, suppliers and clients. The frequent failure of big business to overhaul its procedures in the early 1990s can be attributed to the complexity of the previous technological "client-server architecture" wave. By comparison, transforming such companies today through use of the Internet has become child's play.

By late 2000, four technological trends were contributing to these re-engineering processes:

- A constant reduction in communication costs due to proliferating fibre-optic networks and mushrooming wireless communications.

- New industry-wide standards and protocols, such as HTML, SMTP, FTP, XML, SOAP and UDDL, some imposed by the Internet Society and others established by big players and subsequently released into the public domain.

- New and old Web interfaces and application development tools will greatly simplify the integration of internal data systems with those of clients and partners and will allow industries less involved in information and communications technologies to join in the fray.

- Reduced software and hardware costs, coupled with the open source concept, will take their tolls—exerting downward price pressures on information technology products as a whole.

This set of factors will allow major technological changes to be applied to large corporate information management systems within as little as a few months or a year, compared to three or more years in the past. Since such innovations now include external interfaces, big business is free to disencumber itself of any activities not central to its core goals.

Most analysts concur that vertically integrated companies cannot survive, since the Internet removes the last obstacles to systematic subcontracting. The transfer by large companies of their activities to the Internet is the inevitable consequence of the unrestrained collaborative processes encouraged by B2B e-commerce.

The first experts outside academia to identify collaborative work as the main engine behind B2B were Charles Phillips and Mary Meeker, financial analysts at Morgan Stanley Dean Witter, in *The B2B Internet Report–Collaborative Commerce*. Published just before the Internet bubble burst (which Ms. Meeker helped inflate as a leading dot-com shares expert), their analysis predicts the extinction of any B2B e-marketplaces that confine their role to that of intermediary between buyers and sellers.

Phillips and Meeker noted that the New York Stock Exchange made a mere $101 million U.S. in 1998, despite posting 169 billion transactions valued at $7.3 trillion U.S. They concluded that B2B e-marketplaces with business models based solely on transaction fees could not hope for large revenues. These enterprises must quickly begin offering high-added-value online collaborative resources if they want to grow.

Moving the value chain online

To demonstrate their contention that all industries will ultimately move their values chains into cyberspace, Phillips and Meeker referred to current events in the electronics industry—the heartland of most such change today. Every large computer and communications supplier sub-contracts all or part of its product manufacturing to companies known as Electronic Contract Manufacturers (ECM).

One such subcontractor, Celestica, provides an excellent illustration of this process. Born out of IBM's sell off of two chip manufacturing plants in 1996, this Toronto-based company with two thousand employees at the time grew, through acquisitions, into a multinational firm with a presence on three continents, nineteen thousand employees and thirty plants—in less than five years. While not a typical example of a small business, this case clearly demonstrates the kinds of changes that will affect small suppliers. The roles filled by Celestica and its thirty produc-tion units can easily be filled in other fields by a combination of a e-marketplace or a professional association and small businesses.

Stuck with disparate computer systems, including archaic ERP and in-house solutions, Celestica had to choose between deploying identical applications in all of its divisions or providing a common Web interface through which all of its units—and customers—could access existing systems. Knowing that the second option could be implemented in a matter of months, while refitting standing systems would take at least two years, the Toronto firm did not hesitate.

By making this choice, Celestica not only accelerated its ability to provide manufacturing on demand, it managed to eliminate 80% of manufacturing defects. The time required for production run start-ups was reduced from a week to a day. These improvements were mostly due to Web-based exchanges over a platform known as collaborative product commerce (CPC). One manufacturing-oriented aspect of this CPC process makes it possible to send printed circuit blueprints out for corrections, that do not take Celestica's own manufacturing constraints into account.

Software ready for collaboration

Bruce Bond, a B2B specialist at the Gartner Groups, cites the case of California's Adaptec as another example of the emergence of c-commerce. Linked to its suppliers through a system developed by Extricity that instantly relays any changes in production deadlines, Adaptec can respond appropriately if a situation will affect one of its own customers. Within just one year, this system saved $2 million U.S. in operating costs, has reduced production delays by 40% and has slashed inventory by 25%.

According to Bruce Bond, the Ford Motor Company offers an excellent model of a traditional company with a state-of-the-art electronic strategy. The automaker hosts real-time design sessions with suppliers using digital part models over its Web site. Previously, such collaborative work had been performed by exchanging computer-assisted design (CAD) files, which were then returned following each set of changes. Real-time collaborative design allowed Ford to plan and build its World Car using parts, employees and designers from around the globe.

Technology suppliers were quick to tout the collaborative-friendliness of their products in a rush to embrace this new wave. Lotus, a workgroup software leader, has committed itself to improving the modularity of its products, their compatibility with various major B2B ecommerce standards (including XML) and their integration with its other products, as well as those of third parties. Lotus's goal is to make workflow, online training, document management, application sharing, and other modules plug-and-play ready whenever they are linked to software from Lotus or its partners.

Microsoft is proposing its BizTalk server as a major component of its internet strategy. BizTalk's function is to integrate disparate applications to facilitate internal and external collaboration. In the same spirit, IBM is banking on its WebSphere Studio server. J.D. Edwards is one ERP supplier than has begun knocking on the collaborative door with its launch of OneWorld Xe (for eXtended enterprise), a client relations and logistics chain management suite. One World's main feature is easy integration with a wide variety of other products on the market.

Table 4   The 4 phases of e-commerce

	Phase 1 Batch EDI	Phase 2 Basic E-Commerce	Phase 3 Community Commerce	Phase 4 Collaborative Commerce
Flexibility	Low; rigid format	High; open standards	High; open standards	High; open standards
Costs	High; proprietary network	Low; leverage Internet	Low; leverage Internet	Low; leverage Internet
Business processes supported	Batch orders	Catalog orders	Catalog plus Auction and Bid/Ask	Multiple order forms; B2B interactions
Market transparency	Low; fixed supplier base	Low; no centralized market	High; intergeo-graphy transparency	High; intergeo-graphy transparency

Morgan Stanley Dean Witter, Collaborative Commerce, *April 2000*

Contagious autonomy

These new resources are appealing to, but beyond the financial reach, of many businesses with fewer than 20 employees.

This problem appears to have been solved with the October 2000 launch of Groove[54], the first peer-to-peer communications system dedicated to business applications. It is the first product of Groove Networks, founded in 1997 by Lotus Notes' creator, Ray Ozzie. With the agreement of the two most powerful personalities in the information industry—none other than Bill Gates and Andy Grove – Ozzie claims that software specifically designed for business applications will become as essential as are email and Web-surfing for any private Web surfer.

Peer-to-peer (P2P) communications include all systems in which the brains of a network are located at its extremities—workstations—rather than in its core or on the application servers that form the hubs of the Internet. Some products, like Napster, the music file exchange software, or ICQ's instant messaging software, require some server input. Other products, like Groove, use a pure peer-to-peer model, permitting direct communications between two outlying stations without having to pass through any intermediaries.

Groove's preview edition is free and will be developed into more complex for-sale versions. Groove currently permits basic exchanges (files, lists, message, work schedules, bookmarks, photos, etc.). Collaborative work projects, remote meetings and presentations can also be carried out in Groove's virtual workspaces, reproduced on each participant workstation. Other specialized applications will be grafted to the central core through agreement with a number of partners. Custom functions can be added by selecting appropriate development tools.

Systems like Groove are essential for close collaboration on even moderately complex projects. Email becomes the tool of last resort, because of the vast problems associated with having different versions of a text circulating among many contributors. Teams of up to twenty contributors can easily work over the Groove network because each project is

---

54 Downloadable at www.groove.net

updated on all workstations whenever any contributor connects to the network.

Because of the user independence they encourage and the manner in which they are modelled after naturally overlapping relations between people, P2P networks tend to propagate from a phenomenon known as "viral marketing." Groove and its eventual competitors will likely spread like wildfire among small online businesses and the self-employed, many of which have already signed up to use it—as well as the many multi-disciplinary teams in all big businesses and major organizations.

In contrast with application service providers (ASP), which participate in the traditional computer movement by banking on central control of the final user, P2P communications software is rooted in a combination of distributed data processing and Web user autonomy. Following on the heels of the many remarkable innovations brought about by the Internet, the peer-to-peer concept is demolishing the last bastions of the command and control chain.

Test your knowledge...

To conclude

For a site to be considered an retail e-commerce site, what functionality must absolutely be available?

1. A catalog of products and services and an online purchase form.
2. Access to after-sales service by (800) number, fax, email, ICQ or other.
3. A means by which consumers can provide suggestions and comments about the site, products, etc.
4. A list of distributors and links to their Web site.
5. All of the above.

What new possibility appeared with the advent of technology that accelerated it's usage as well as its penetration in the market?

1. Teams can be made up and disbanded according to specific projects.
2. Buying decisions can be made in real time.
3. Resources can be found for free.
4. Free services can be offered to help sell others that are income-generating.
5. Alliances can be made with competitors.

GLOSSARY

ASP
Application Service Providers. A company that lets customers at distant locations access specialized software applications hosted on its servers, generally over the Internet.

Attachment
A text, image, sound or other document attached to an email but opened separately from it by the recipient.

B2B e-commerce
Electronic commerce between businesses, aimed at exchanging goods and services by means of EDI systems, or over extranets and VPNs. Particularly popular in the supply sector and in dealings between large customers and their many small suppliers (as in the automotive and aviation industries).

B2G
E-commerce between business and government. It may include tax payments or refunds, the procurement of goods and services or the provision of governmental services (issuance of licences, permits, statistical information and so forth).

Banner ad
A type of online classified ad usually placed at the top of a Web page, consisting of an image or brief message inviting visitors to click through to the advertising site.

Cracker
Computer and network enthusiast who takes pleasure in penetrating server or site defences, often with malevolent intent.

CRM
Customer Relationship Management applications help manage customer relations, particularly over the Internet.

Cross-certification
Authentication of two or more parties not physically present for a transaction, as by certification authorities in different countries.

Cryptography
Set of technologies used to encode and decode messages to make them impenetrable. Basic principles go back as far as the Roman Empire. Modern use dates from work performed by the Germans (Enigma) and the British (Ultra and Alan Turing) prior to and during World War II.

Cybernotaries
Notaries or officers of the law considered good candidates in many countries (including the U.S.) to serve as trusted third parties (TTP) for international commercial transactions.

Cyberspace law
New legal speciality covering issues specific to the Internet in general and to ecommerce in particular. This involves fields such as intellectual property of domain names, protection of privacy, electronic contracts and electronic signatures, justiciability (or the ability to bring a matter before a court), voluntary arbitration, and so forth.

Cyberspace
The "ether", or imaginary space in which the Internet exists and in which Web surfers indulge in various activities.

Data mining
The ability to extract and combine disparate data from a variety of sources to obtain useful information on markets, customers, how a company operates and so forth. This technique may raise ethical and confidentiality issues when it uses data collected without the consent or knowledge of users and consumers, particularly from Web sites.

Digital signature
Phrase or signature encrypted using a signatory's private key. By decoding this message with the sender's public key, the recipient can be certain it has been sent from the proper party. Biometric methods are also available for identification.

Disintermediation
A big word hiding a simple reality: media convergence and networking have tended to bypass conventional business relations and are causing traditional intermediaries to fade away.

Domain name
Address of an Internet-based machine or sub-network. Such addresses are hosted in Domain Name Servers (DNS). Domain addresses are formed from a set of abbreviations or words separated by dots, based on international conventions.

Dot.com
Emerging Internet-based companies that do most of their business online.

E-business

Business model that integrates the Internet into a company's activities. There are three main types of e-business activities: e-commerce, B2B collaboration and customer service. The development of ebusiness is closely linked to the that of intranets and extranets. E-business should help companies share information more quickly and efficiently, thus boosting their growth and competitiveness.

E-business

IBM's term designed to expand the concept of electronic commerce from mere transactions to all economic relations between businesses, institutions and government agencies operating over the Internet or its variants (intranets, extranets and VPNs). This includes bidding, calls for tenders, tax payments or refunds, electronic contracts, job hunting or staffing, free or paid subscriptions and so forth.

EDI

Electronic Document Interchange. A system that makes it possible to exchange computer-readable forms. Used to automate various aspects of B2B exchanges.

Electronic Commerce or e-commerce

The purchase and sale of goods and services over a digital network (the Internet). To qualify as e-commerce, an entire transaction including delivery, or just one of its facets (consultation of a catalogue, ordering, payment, follow-up on delivery, etc.), must occur online (while the rest can be performed by conventional means).

Electronic markets

The physical chain of distribution is gradually yielding to a commercial cyberspace of online transactions. The prediction by MIT's Tom Malone that corporations will shrink as e-marketplaces grow is coming true. Furthermore, new virtual products are being offered on these markets, such as bandwidth reservations and "pollution rights."

Email
Electronic mail is a system enabling two parties to swap messages over the Internet almost instantaneously. Each party has an email box addressed in the form of name@server.type. Generally, plain text makes up the body of an email, but pictures, spreadsheets, video or sounds clips may also be sent as "attachments."

E-marketplace
Web site used for e-commerce, particularly between businesses, where visitors can select goods or services and make secure online payments. E-marketplaces can be organized to serve horizontal (a range of industries), vertical (a single industry), geographic and mass market customer bases.

Encryption
Technical term for encoding documents to make them impenetrable.

E-newsletter
Virtual publication to which Web site visitors may subscribe, to obtain emailed updates on current site topics.

ERP
Entreprise Resource Planning. Complex corporate management application, particularly used for managing human resources, equipment and facilities.

E-tailing
Retail business-to-consumer or consumer-to-consumer online ecommerce (as found on auction sites).

Extranet
Private and confidential network linking two or more businesses, running on Internet-based tools and protocols. Extranets are often used to communicate between two or more intranets (see below).

Firewall
Server designed to protect a network connected to the Internet from hacking.

Groupware
Groupware permits a group of people to work together from separate locations. Lotus Notes and Microsoft NetMeeting are the best-known applications of this kind.

Hacker
Resourceful and imaginative computer enthusiast, as distinguished from "cracker" (expert in cracking protected sites and software). Hackers may, however, also be crackers.

HTML
HyperText Markup Language. A computer language used to produce Web pages.

Intranet
Private and confidential internal network running on Internet-based protocols and tools. Also see "extranet."

Key escrow
System in which a trusted depository holds the private keys of all parties to a public-key encryption system. In the event of a criminal or legal action, a private key may be revealed to the appropriate authorities if a warrant is issued or under other circumstances pursuant to law, to permit decoding of suspect messages.

Knowledge management
Information and knowledge are critical resources in the New Economy and must be managed like all other resources. Although the principle is simple and logical, its application is much less clear. "Knowledge Management" has become a buzzword covering technologies and approaches as disparate as competitive intelligence, data mining, expert systems and so forth.

LINUX

Free UNIX-based operating system distributed on the general public licence (GPL) principle. The fact that LINUX is free has contributed to its success, as well as the fact it runs on various platforms, including the PC, Macintosh and Amiga. Each LINUX version is called a "distribution."

Mass customization

The industrial revolution made possible the production of large numbers of identical products at low cost . . . and small numbers of "customized" products at very high cost. Now, new technologies are making it possible to combine the best of both worlds, by producing goods tailored to the needs or desires of individual buyers at reasonable prices. For example, anyone can now order a "factory" Ford, with all desired options, and have it delivered to the nearest dealer.

Middleware

Specialized software used to integrate a firm's legacy systems with new Internet and ecommerce applications.

Network externalities

Situation when use of a product, a resource or a software application by a large numbers of people over a network gives it greater value and encourages other users to adopt it. Such a situation could, ultimately, create a monopoly.

Non-repudiation

The process whereby an encrypted message bundled with an electronic signature ensures both parties that a communication has not been altered, while also confirming the identities of originator and recipient. Evidence of a message's non-repudiability must be rigourous if it is to be submitted in court.

Online advertising

Set of visual, auditory and sometimes interactive Web-based media used to provide information to consumers and urge them to buy a particular product or service online. Banner ads and broadcast emailings are two of the chief methods employed.

Online Auction

Web site hosting auctions over the Internet in which a number of individuals or companies compete to buy a particular product or service, which is ultimately sold to the highest bidder.

Online community

Web site enabling individuals or companies sharing common interests to come into contact so they can exchange information, goods or services.

Online marketing

Use of new communications and IT technologies, such as the Internet, for market studies, sales and promotion.

Portal

A Web site that can be used as a point of entry and access ramp to a range of other Web sites and online services. A portal may serve the general public, a single industry (vertical), a country or region (geographic) or the business community.

Private key

A user's "private" key in the asymmetric or "public key" cryptographic system. As this key is never transmitted over the network, the security of such a system is greater than that of a symmetrical "secret key" system.

Public key system

System in which two "linked" keys exist for each user—one to encrypt and the other to decrypt the same message. One such key is private, while the other is public and can be looked up like in a directory, just like a phone number. In this way the private key is never transmitted, and security is much tighter than with "secret key" systems. With a bi-directional algorithm, each key can both encode and decode messages. This makes it possible to encrypt non-repudiable signature codes and allow even parties unknown to each other to engage in confidential exchanges and transactions.

Referencing
Also known as listing. Listing a Web site in various search engines to increase visibility among Web users and boost traffic. To list a site, a Webmaster submits its URL (Universal Resource Locator), an email contact address and possibly other information, such as site name, site description, site category, keywords and so forth. With the proliferation in number of sites, site listing has become a mini-industry in the hands of experts who charge for their services.

Reverse auction
An online auction in which buyers dictate terms (including prices) and suppliers compete for orders. Priceline.com introduced this sort of e-tailing to the Web.

Search engine (site)
Software that uses a predefined format to generate a list of Web addresses, or URLs (Uniform Resource Locators) with contents matching search criteria. A search engine retrieves submitted terms from indexes previously created through constant consultation of Web sites around the world. AltaVista, Yahoo!, Infoseek and Lycos are a few popular search engines.

Secret key
In a symmetric cryptographic system, a message is encrypted using the same "key" held by the recipient to decode the message. This key must be transmitted separately from the message to decrease the risk of misuse.

Secure message
Text encrypted using a recipient's public key, which can then only be
decoded with the latter's private key.

Secure Payment
Online Internet-based payment using a secure encryption protocol.

Security
Broad term pertaining to all aspects of e-commerce that can affect
the confidence of users and companies. Pertains to the confidentiality
and reliability of transactions, the identities of distant parties to such
transactions and so forth. There are three main aspects of security. They
are technological (encryption and e-signatures), legal (non-repudiation,
validity of contracts and documents) and structural (trusted third parties, directories and depositories of encryption keys).

Server
Computer running specialized applications that provide network-based
user services.

Spam
Term for a flood of unsolicited promotional email.

Supply Chain
The set of operations accompanying and following a sale, including
inventory management, order management, wrapping, delivery, war-
ranty service, etc.

Supply Value Chain
Set of economic relationships maintained by various parties to a transaction, starting with extraction of raw materials and concluding with the
delivery of a finished product to an end user.

Telecommuting

Enables employees and associates to work from remote locations (such as the home) over the Internet or some other network, with the same access to company systems as if they were in the workplace.

Transactional site

Site permitting online commercial or financial transactions involving payment by credit card, bank transfer or e-money. Requires specialized software and enhanced security.

Trusted Third Party

TTP. An intermediary with many roles, all involving confidentiality and reliability. In escrow systems, the TTP holds codes, which may only be revealed to the proper authorities as provided by law. In "open" commercial transactions, the TTP identifies and serves as guarantor of each party. In "closed" public key transactions, the TTP merely confirms the status or solvency of the contracting parties.

Value added network

VAN. A private network running on a medium other than the Internet and offering additional features. Up until now, VANs have served as the main gateways for electronic business-to-business dealings, particularly with respect to EDI transactions.

Virtual Private Network

Software installed on two or more systems permits private and transparent exchanges of information. Through sophisticated encryption and security techniques, users enjoy the benefits of a private network, while actually using a public one (typically the Internet).

Virus

Generally a small program that invisibly lodges itself within a computer connected to the Internet or some other network and performs a variety of activities, most of which are harmful to the computing system. Many viruses can automatically reproduce and thus proliferate through a vast number of systems. Various means of protection, known as anti-virus applications, are available.

Web Hosting
Storing a document or a Web site on a server for diffusion over the Internet. Many companies prefer third-party hosting to avoid the technical problems and management costs associated with maintaining their own servers.

Web
Or World Wide Web, the graphic, hypertext and most popular branch of the Internet, consisting of a vast number of interlinked servers with contents coded primarily in the HTML language, and accessible through clickable links. The Web can be navigated using browsers, such as Internet Explorer and Netscape. This is the preferred domain of ecommerce. A set of Web pages devoted to a particular subject, institution or company is known as a "site."

XML
Expandable Markup Language, a computer language used, like HTML, to write Web pages, but different from the latter because the programmer can create specific "types" and dynamic elements.

I am delighted to announce the release of the Winning Strategy for B2B E-Commerce, a reference work designed to guide small businesses seeking to expand into ebusiness activities.

This text is particularly useful in that it will help small businesses integrate new Internet-based and information technologies with their in-house practices, making them that much more competitive and productive. With that in mind, I would like to invite Quebec's small businesses to move up to this next level of doing business.

The Electronic Commerce Institute seeks to extend Government of Quebec efforts geared to supporting growth in electronic business practices. We hope this work will help provide the kinds of benefits that make Quebec more completely wired to the needs of business than ever before!

David Cliche

Minister Responsible for the Information Highway and Governmental Services

Québec 🏵🏵🏵🏵

**Secrétariat
du Conseil du trésor**

**Subventionné par le
Fonds de l'autoroute de l'information**

QuébecTel management is proud to be working in partnership with the Electronic Commerce Institute, the Business Development Bank of Canada and Cogitex to offer Quebec small businesses a practical guide to business-to-business e-commerce (B2B).

After all is said and done, e-commerce is still business, which means a set of relationships designed to meet individual, corporate and collective needs. However, because e-commerce runs on an electronic platform, an arsenal of information, communications and technology (ICT) tools supplement the traditional ways of doing business.

While e-commerce shares the same ultimate goals of traditional business, it employs new means of achieving them. The medium is the message and different forms of communications are changing the way business is done. In other words, we may be able to alter reality by the manner in which we perceive and manage it. Emerging forms of business are thus extending our concepts of time and space by placing much greater emphasis on knowledge and information. This process may ultimately reshuffle the relationships of power among different businesses.

Common sense will always be important in business, and common sense demands that each decision-maker carefully gauge the pluses and minuses inherent in the range of ecommerce applications. We believe this guide will enciourage such common sense among Quebec's professional workers and small business operators and help them select the right e-business solutions.

QuébecTel and its subsidiaries are striving to bolster the success of the companies and organizations with which they do business. That is why we are offering companies of every size, in any industry and in all areas, a full and integrated range of e-business solutions for doing better business reliably, effectively and securely.

We hope you will include this guide among your valued reference tools—and use it to better understand and manage your new ways of doing business.

Hugues St-Pierre
President QuébecTel

Electronic commerce, almost inconceivable less than 10 years ago is, with lightning speed, becoming an essential component of economic activity worldwide. In Canada, the total value of customer orders received over the Internet, with or without online payment, was $4.4 billion in 1999. That same year, 53% of private sector enterprises used the Internet in one form or another.

For businesses wishing to develop new markets or expand existing ones, these figures clearly demonstrate the importance of becoming familiar with the benefits of electronic commerce, especially business to business (B2B) e-commerce. By answering a wide variety of questions about cybercommerce, this guide will help enterprises take full advantage of the phenomenal growth of online transactions.

As Minister of National Revenue and Secretary of State responsible for Canada Economic Development, I salute this Electronic Commerce Institute initiative, which will facilitate Quebec SMEs' transition from the traditional to the virtual world of business.

Martin Cauchon

Canada Economic Development   Développement économique Cana

Canada

Globalization, cyber-commerce and technological advances are the driving forces of today's business world. The companies that adapt to these realities through the use of leading-edge productivity tools are the ones that succeed in the new economy.

Fortunately, the time is ripe for Canadian businesses to invest in productivity-enhancing e-commerce tools. Recent innovations in this relatively new and rapidly evolving domain have produced a wide range of economical solutions adapted to the needs of today's businesses. Innovative e-commerce strategies are now helping businesses become more competitive by allowing them to work smarter and expand their reach into new markets.

This guide contains valuable information about doing business online, designed to make the challenges of e-commerce and enhanced productivity a little easier. The Business Development Bank of Canada (BDC), in business for small business, is pleased to support this Electronic Commerce Institute initiative as a means of helping Canadian small businesses take advantage of the full potential of the global Internet economy.

Michel Vennat
President and Chief Executive Officer

BDC

Business Development Bank of Canada
Banque de développement du Canada